The ⌐
of My ⌐

The private prayers of public people,
chosen for BBC Radio 4

JAMES WHITBOURN

TRIANGLE

First published in Great Britain 1997

Triangle Books
Holy Trinity Church
Marylebone Road
London NW1 4DU

Published by arrangement with the BBC. This book is
based on the BBC Radio series, *Prayer for the Day*.
Prayer for the Day is a BBC trade mark.

British Library Cataloguing-in-Publication Data

A catalogue record of this book is available
from the British Library

ISBN 0–281–05022–8

Typeset by Pioneer Associates, Perthshire
Printed in Great Britain by
Caledonian International, Glasgow

For my parents, with love

Contents

THE BEST OF MY BELIEF

James Whitbourn has presented BBC Radio 4's *Prayer for the Day* every Saturday since March 1989. In addition to the weekly interview, he produces and presents many programmes for BBC Radio and Television, including *Choral Evensong*, of which he is Series Producer, and *Carols from King's*. He is also a Director of Music for the *Daily Service*. His previous books include *A Prayer in the Life* (Triangle 1993) and *In Tuneful Accord* (SPCK 1996). James and his wife, Alison, live in Kent with their two daughters, Hannah and Naomi.

Also by James Whitbourn and published by
Triangle and SPCK:

A Prayer in the Life (Triangle 1993)

In Tuneful Accord (SPCK 1996)

Introduction

'Do you know anything about eternal life?' says the woman on the BBC switchboard, 'only I've got a listener here asking about it.' For a moment I wonder whether there is a new pop group of that name, which has escaped my notice. Maybe the listener wanted to speak to Youth Programmes on the floor below? 'Okay, put her through.'

No, she had wanted to speak to me. She had stumbled across something on the radio last Saturday morning which caused her to think again about the ultimate truths, and she thought I might have the answers. Unfortunately, I did not. One of my guests had said something which opened her understanding of God in a way which she had never experienced before, and she wanted to know more. I suggest she makes a date with the programme every Saturday morning. No one person holds all the truths, I explain, but each individual adds a tiny piece to the jigsaw, and you find a picture begins to emerge.

A few months later, the same woman telephones again. She has listened every week since that first conversation. She has got the corner pieces in place, she tells me, and is working her way into the middle of the puzzle.

The presenter of Saturday morning *Prayer for the Day* is in a privileged position. Usually, when people meet for the first time, they chat about the route they took, the weather or some insignificant detail of mundane life. Meeting someone to record an edition of the Radio 4 programme is a different matter. After arriving at the house, and maybe enjoying a coffee together, we turn swiftly to the innermost feelings and begin to discuss the deepest personal beliefs. It is the sort of conversation that many close friends never have at all, and that others have not experienced since those late nights they used to have in their student days, when talk turned to religion at about two o'clock in the morning.

For some, a deeply held conviction is based upon a lifetime's experience. It is said that as people get older, they believe more and more in less and less. In time, their true beliefs become progressively clearer, and at some point it

1

becomes possible to distil their convictions into a single prayer, inspired by a lifetime of searching in faith.

When I telephone people to invite them on to the programme, I ask them to choose a prayer. But I explain that I use the term in its widest sense, meaning any text which inspires a particular communion with or connection to God. It does not have to be a prayer in the formal sense of one addressed directly to God, and many have chosen passages of Scripture, or simple meditations which focus their thoughts powerfully upon their creator. The Book of Psalms is an eternally rich source for such meditations, and it is well represented in this collection.

Every week, listeners write to the *Prayer for the Day* office asking for copies of the prayers used. They have heard them in the 6.50 a.m. broadcast, and would like a copy to reflect upon them at greater length. That is the purpose of this second collection published by Triangle – a companion volume to *A Prayer in the Life*, based upon the same idea, and which was brought out in 1993.

Any collection which involves so many people must be regarded as a combined effort, and I am grateful to the producers, researchers and production assistants who have worked on Saturday *Prayer for the Day* over the last few years. Many colleagues, as well as friends and family, have suggested possible guests to me, for which I am also grateful.

Thanks are also due to Rachel Boulding, formerly of SPCK, who was involved in the publication of the first collection four years ago, and encouraged me to embark upon this one.

There is a good deal of careful work which goes into the preparation of even a short book such as this – scores of letters to contributors, publishers, copyright holders and the like – not to mention the heavy task of transcribing interviews from recorded tapes. All this has been done by Sue Hewett, to whom I owe enormous thanks.

Above all, my thanks go to the fifty-three guests who have allowed me to retell our conversations in this book. They have offered insight and understanding, and I am delighted that their thoughts and prayers can now be kept and reread.

JAMES WHITBOURN

The private prayers of public people,
chosen for BBC Radio 4

David Adam

Planning a journey to Holy Island is a precision task. Every day, at different times, the long causeway which leads out from the mainland is covered with sea, leaving Lindisfarne truly an island. It is a fact which must have ensured its long history as a holy place of pilgrimage and retreat. My journey is to meet the vicar of Holy Island, one of the foremost writers of modern Celtic poetry. The prayer which David Adam has chosen itself plays on the image of an island.

'It is about the feeling first, that sometimes we are down, life is hard and we are in the dark. Second, it is about the reality that, behind those feelings, there is something rather wonderful happening and we are not left alone.

'Like any human being, I have had quite a few grim moments and cheerless days. I have to teach myself, quite often, that the path of light is still there. No matter what I feel like, I am not forsaken.'

'Where do you find that path of light?'

'That is hard to describe. There is an experience which I had quite often when I lived on the moors. My house was in the fog, and I could drive my car to the moor top and look down on the fog. We have the ability as human beings to step out of one experience we are going through into something totally different.'

Something unusual has struck me about this prayer. When it speaks of greatness and glory, it refers not to God, but to the one who prays to God. What sort of greatness would David Adam claim as his own?

'That I am a son of God. If I had been a female I would say that I am a daughter of God. We are God's creation, he loves us, cares for us, is with us and upholds us. Surely if you believe all of that, there is a greatness going on in your life which makes you rather great. The feeling comes by spending as much time as I can just being happily in the presence, without doing anything other than that. If you want an image, it is a bit like sunbathing. If you know the sun is there, you can relax and enjoy it.

'So I would happily say "I am on my way to thy glory". Not

4

in the sense of being absolutely confident where I will end up, but in the belief that, if we are striving to be towards God, God moves so close that glory is all about us and very near. Perhaps I am still blind, but because it is there, I am in it, and you are in it. We are all in glory.'

The Revd David Adam is Vicar of Holy Island. He was a coalminer before being ordained. During his twenty years as Vicar of Danby, North Yorkshire, he began composing prayers in the Celtic pattern, and has published several popular collections since.

Though the dawn breaks cheerless on this Isle today,
My spirit walks upon a path of light.
For I know my greatness.
Thou has built me a throne within thy heart.
I dwell safely within the circle of thy care.
I cannot for a moment fall out of thy everlasting arms
I am on my way to thy glory.

Alaistair Maclean

Richard Addis

Lucinda was thirty-two years old. Two weeks after her wedding day, she died. The young woman had once been secretary to Richard Addis, now editor of the *Express*. His glass office overlooks the Thames, and he glances over in the direction of St Paul's Cathedral as he recalls why he had turned to the words of Alcuin, the eighth-century Archbishop of York, in such tragic circumstances.

'I chose the poem and read it at her funeral in order to try to say to her husband and her parents that her death was not completely the end of everything, and certainly was not the end of her love for her husband. After that, I realized it was a poem not just about lovers, but about friends, God and our relationship with God.'

The opening lines seem to allude to something which goes beyond death. What is it?

'Love – in the Christian sense, that is, not the modern romantic and rather pathetic newspaper sense.' This from a tabloid editor? He laughs and acknowledges the irony of what he has just said. 'The trouble is that most people, when they talk about love, mean little more than a flush of passion or some exciting feeling – which is very sad. Love is really about a deep and abiding friendship and loyalty. Christian theology understands that and when great writers write about the love of God, they define it in the most absolute and rock-like terms. If one can experience any form of love which is anything approximating to that kind of firm and lasting love, then one is very lucky.'

Alcuin's lines have many possible meanings. They could, I suggest, be about love, death, the afterlife, or all of these.

'I agree with you that they are about many things. The phrase "see each other face to face" is a way of talking about seeing the true character of the other person unadorned and without any distraction. But it is also partly about what might happen with one's relationship with God, in which one has all sorts of interruptions, acclusions, difficulties and sub-versions, and the Christian hope is that, at the end, you get a chance to see what you have been about all through your life, absolutely clearly and unadorned. The final line of the poem again rather cleverly implies the possibility that, because emotions do not matter, if you love someone very deeply then you do not have all this rushing of blood to the head, but can feel you have just one heart which joins you.'

'Is this an allusion also to a relationship with God?'

'I think it works on both levels. Really good human friends are very much like human relationships with God. The nearest thing anyone gets to understanding what it might be like to have a very profound saint-like relationship with God is to have a friend.'

Richard Addis, a former novice in an Anglican order, held posts at the Evening Standard *and* Sunday Telegraph *before becoming Associate Editor of the* Daily Mail *and Editor of the* Express.

Come, make an end of singing and of grieving,
But not an end of love.
I wrote this song, beloved, bitter, weeping,
And yet I know 'twill prove
That by God's grace,
We two shall see each other face to face,
And stand together with a heart at rest.

Alcuin (*c.*735–804)

Ossie Ardiles

At the start of a new football season, White Hart Lane has a buzz of excitement. The German footballer Jurgen Klinsmann has just arrived to join Tottenham Hotspur Football Club. He is busy shaking hands with his future colleagues as I slip past into the office of the manager who has signed him. Ossie Ardiles believes in beautiful football – a game for the spectator as well as for the players and managers. The 1994 season is a time of promise and excitement for the London club, and spirits are high. All the more surprising, perhaps, that the Spurs' manager should have chosen a text which begins 'Blessed are the poor in spirit: for theirs is the kingdom of heaven.'

'I believe that this is a wonderful message of hope more than anything else. It gives hope even when you think that everything in your life is going wrong. Sometimes you feel you have this message of hope at the end of the day, and that is the wonderful beauty of it.

'To people who feel very superior – "kings" or "important people" in this world who sometimes feel like that, or who have the world in their hands – I say it is never like that. And Jesus shows that the number one in the kingdom of God is the one who is a servant. The last in this world will be the first in the kingdom of God.'

Footballers, it must be said, are not poor. Even lowly players work on huge salaries, and the Premier League is the richest in the world. I ask him how he squares all this with the message of the passage.

'I don't see any conflict at all. The fact that you are lucky to have certain material things does not give you the licence to do whatever you want to do. On the contrary, they give you more and more responsibility to do the right thing. It probably matters more when things are going really well because then you read something like that and say, "I don't have to be that big, I don't have to be thinking so elated." If you win a game, for example, or you are a champion, however beautiful this thing could be, the most important thing of all is your relationship with your creator.'

'Do you see dangers when you are "on a high" professionally and in other ways?'

'Yes, because when you are on a high, it is much easier to forget God. When you are in need, and when things are not going your way, then it is much, much easier to pray, and much easier to be with God. So these words of Jesus are not so much for the people who are poor in spirit or humble, but, on the contrary, for people who are on a big high in this world. He is saying to them, "you do not need to be like that because *you* are not the blessed one, but the other guy".'

Ossie Ardiles won forty-two international caps for Argentina, with whom he was a World Cup winner in 1978. He played 238 League games for Tottenham Hotspur between 1978–88, returning briefly as Spurs' manager from June 1993 to October 1994.

Blessed are the poor in spirit: for theirs is the kingdom
of heaven.
Blessed are they that mourn: for they shall be comforted.
Blessed are the meek: for they shall inherit the earth.
Blessed are they which do hunger and thirst after
righteousness: for they shall be filled.
Blessed are the merciful: for they shall obtain mercy.
Blessed are the pure in heart: for they shall see God.
Blessed are the peacemakers: for they shall be called
the children of God.
Blessed are they which are persecuted for righteousness'
sake: for theirs is the kingdom of heaven.

Matthew 5.3–10
(Authorized Version)

Revd W. Awdry

It seems strange to be addressing as 'Father Wilbert' someone only ever known by his initial. The Revd W. Awdry obligingly signs one of my daughter's Thomas the Tank Engine books and looks almost embarrassed as he hands it back. The success of his little stories has left him completely unchanged. A modest terraced house still sees him good. Sitting in a rather upright chair, he keeps in easy reach anything he might need. 'My only luxury is a housekeeper', he explains as she brings in tea. 'All through my ministerial life I've tried to help people to see God in ordinary everyday things.' Ordinary in outward appearance, perhaps, but the Revd W. Awdry has a remarkable youthfulness for an old man. He is a born story-teller, and it seems absolutely right that I should be asking him about one of Jesus' stories – that of the lost coin.

'These parables which our Lord told of lost things reflect God's love to us, so we are seeing God in ordinary everyday life. God is more human than we suppose, and he has an all-embracing love for everything that he has created. He loves us just as we love our possessions. This instinct is implanted in us and I once had an exasperating illustration of it. My daughter and my granddaughter came to stay – the little girl was about two and she had what had been one of her earliest presents, a woolly rabbit. Now, by the time she was two years old, this rabbit ceased to be really like a rabbit – it was absolutely disreputable – but it was a most treasured possession and she always went to bed with it. One day rabbit could not be found. The whole house was turned upside down to find this wretched rabbit but the little girl stood at the top of the stairs – "I want my wabbit!". When she was offered a substitute – "that's not my wabbit!". At last she was coaxed by her mother to get into bed and then my wife had time to unpack the shopping trolley. There at the bottom was "wabbit".

'You should have seen the joy on that child's face – from woebegotten, she was grinning all over her face. We have laughed about it afterwards. But to me it brought back the humanity of the search.'

'So, is God seeking to win back every sinner?'

'Yes, and he relies on us to help him do it. When it is achieved, there is joy in heaven.'

The Revd W. Awdry's stories of Thomas the Tank Engine and friends have delighted children for more than fifty years. He died in March 1997.

What woman, having ten silver coins,
if she loses one coin,
does not light a lamp and sweep the house
and seek diligently until she finds it?
And when she has found it,
she calls together her friends and neighbours, saying,
'Rejoice with me for I have found the coin which I
    had lost'.
Just so, I tell you,
there is joy before the angels of God over one
    sinner who repents.

Luke 15. 8–10
(Revised Standard Version)

Sister Wendy Beckett

The setting is a small Carmelite monastery in Norfolk. I have gone there to meet a contemplative nun whose first seventeen years there were spent as a hermit, emerging from her caravan in the woods only to attend Mass and to eat. That was before the media discovered her interest in art, her love of which is now known to millions through books and television programmes. She tells me about a prayer she had written all those years ago at the start of her new life in the monastery.

'I wanted to make a prayer that would express completely what I wanted my life to be. I was starting a new life of living in complete solitude as a hermit, with seven hours of prayer a day, and I did not want any of that to be wasted. This prayer is like an arrow. I think about what matters to me in life, and then try to arrow myself straight to God, on the lines that this prayer suggests. Because we are weak and human, we live in a placid sort of way most of the time. But if we can have worked out once what we essentially want, then we just have to put our hand on it to recall it, and this prayer was, for me, what I was all about.'

The prayer is about the total 'Yes' of Jesus to the Father. How near to the goal does she get?

'Only Jesus can say that total Yes. Do you remember what it says in the Scripture – only Yes was in him. That has always struck me as one of the most wonderful phrases in the whole of the Epistles. Now, in us you see part Yes and part No. We would like it to be all Yes but we are just not able to do it because, at levels we cannot even reach, there are parts of us that do not belong to the Father. So it is no good my trying to say a total Yes because I have not got a totality of Yes to say. But Jesus said a total Yes, and that was what I wanted – everything given.'

The purpose of her prayer is that this Yes should be uttered for the whole world. Why not just for herself?

'I don't think anything is ever given just for self and if we are given prayer, we are given it for everybody. Some people have a vocation to do a lot practically. My vocation, like those of all contemplative sisters, is to do a lot spiritually to make certain that everything God gives is received gratefully and used for others. I cannot fulfil the total Yes – that is the point of the prayer. It is the Spirit of Jesus who prays that total Yes, so the prayer begins with an offering of my own – my poor mean self to that Spirit, who alone is able to say the Yes of Jesus.'

Sister Wendy Beckett is a contemplative nun who lives in seclusion in the grounds of a Carmelite monastery in Norfolk. She was educated at Oxford University where she was awarded a Congratulatory First in English. A lifelong art lover, she began to devote herself to studying it in 1980 and has written many books on the subject.

Come Holy Spirit;
utter within me for the whole world,
the total
Yes
of Jesus
to the Father.

Sister Wendy Beckett

Dickie Bird

There were a few overs before the end of play when I arrived at the Canterbury ground. The locals, who had made a day of it, knew precisely how many balls were left, and were poised, autograph books in hand. As the stumps were wrenched from the ground, in they swarmed to try their luck. The players quickly found their way to the pavilion, and, after a few minutes, only one man dressed in white remained, surrounded by enthusiastic cricketers. The umpire. Dickie Bird is surely the best-loved umpire, not only of cricket but of any sport. Eventually, I manage to get myself near. 'Just let me have a shower,' he says, 'and I'll be right with you.' The umpires' room looks out over the green pastures of the Kent ground. His hair dripping a little, the legendary sportsman surveys the scene as he ponders the words of Psalm 23 in his thick Yorkshire tones.

'My father loved this psalm. When he went down the mine, he always used to say "The Lord is my shepherd: therefore can I lack nothing." And when he went down that mine, same as when I go on to a cricket ground, he always said the Lord was with him. And when he was down the mine at the coal-face he always said that the Lord was with him there as well.

'You see, I have a tremendous faith and I thank the Lord for giving me a gift. He gave me this gift to play county cricket and to umpire 159 international matches, and I am so grateful and thankful to him. He has given me something in life – the chance to meet some wonderful people and I am so grateful to him for everything that I achieved in the sporting world.'

This psalm, I add, is also about protection. Does that have resonance too?

'Yes it has, because I'll always remember when my father was on his deathbed, and also my mum, when they were on their deathbeds – they said to me, "Carry on as you are; you are doing very well in the sporting world." They said, when they got to heaven (and I know they are in heaven because they had tremendous faith) they would look down on me and see what I am doing in the test match arenas, and would get a lot of pleasure. I feel protected. Every morning I get down on my knees and I pray. Every evening I get down on my knees and I pray. And when I go out there into the middle, I feel protected because I know, and I have faith, that the good Lord is at my side. And I look back, going right back now throughout my life from childhood to now, and this psalm covers everything in it. And you know, when I read this psalm I have a lump in my throat, and it brings tears to my eyes. And I'm not afraid to admit it.'

Dickie (Harold) Bird, Test cricket umpire, retired in 1996.

The Lord is my shepherd: therefore can I lack nothing.

He shall feed me in a green pasture:
and lead me forth beside the waters of comfort.

He shall convert my soul:
and bring me forth in the paths of righteousness,
    for his name's sake.

Yea, though I walk through the valley of the shadow
    of death, I will fear no evil:
for thou art with me; thy rod and thy staff comfort me.

Thou shalt prepare a table before me against them that
    trouble me:
thou hast anointed my head with oil,
and my cup shall be full.

But thy loving-kindness and mercy shall follow me all the
    days of my life: and I will dwell in the house of the
    Lord for ever.

Psalm 23
Book of Common Prayer (1662)

Tony Blair

People are always suspicious of politicians, and never more so than when they speak of their religious convictions. The cynics are inclined to put any such utterings down to point scoring or vote winning. To that extent, I am glad I met Tony Blair long before he became Leader of the Labour Party. I meet him as Home Affairs Spokesman, and, with John Smith relatively newly at the helm and apparently in good health, no one expects any move for some considerable time. His office is situated across the road from the Houses of Parliament, and I am there to hear why he has made such a dramatic choice of prayer – Bonhoeffer's words on the eve of his execution.

'I've chosen the poem by Bonhoeffer for three reasons: first, because I immensely admire the man and the tremendous courage he showed in the face of his impending execution in a Nazi prison camp. Second, because in the face of this ordeal he is not turning in on himself. It is not an introspective poem – he is reaching out beyond himself. Third, I think it is a very humble poem. It catches the essence of humility for me because he acknowledges the precariousness of his situation and yet he has faith that, in the end, that is the right thing for him to do.'

Bonhoeffer's prayer is a poem of contrasts: darkness with light and restlessness with peace.

'I draw strength from the extremes of possibility, because I think the prayer is really about his own objective situation, which is obviously hopeless. He is awaiting execution, feels bitter, weak and deserted, yet has this inner strength – faith – that, in the end, this is the best for him. It is the thing that he *should* be doing and he conquers his own situation through that faith. I think that that is an immensely powerful image.

'When you look around the world today, you see millions of people starving, you see war and whole continents ravaged by internal dissent and conflict. It is very easy to think that the situation is utterly hopeless. Yet what comes through the prayers and poems of all great men like Bonhoeffer is this enormous sense that there is an imperative within you to strive to improve the situation. It may seem hopeless but it is not. It is with hope, because it is always worth striving to improve.'

We come to the sentence 'Thy ways are past understanding, but thou knowest the way for me.' It seems almost unreasonable confidence in the face of uncertainty.

'I share the desire to have confidence. I should imagine that he was racked with doubt all the way through. What makes it a prayer is that, when he comes to it, he *has* faith when this is what faith is about. He believes that, even though he cannot understand what is happening in the world, and even though he can see no logic or reason in it, none the less there is a purpose, and that he has his place within that purpose. And I believe it is a humble prayer because it recognizes the incredible feebleness of the human situation, but sees beyond it. He has faith that things will work out, but no certain knowledge in the practical way that people talk about it. That, to me, is what the mystery of faith is all about.'

Tony Blair has been Prime Minister of Great Britain since May 1997.

In me there is darkness, but with thee there is light.
I am lonely, but thou leavest me not;
I am feeble in heart, but thou leavest me not;
I am restless, but with thee there is peace,
In me there is bitterness, but with thee there is patience.
Thy ways are past understanding, but thou knowest
    the way for me.

Dietrich Bonhoeffer (1906–45)
from a prayer written while awaiting execution in
a Nazi prison

Katie Boyle

It is an odd time to arrange an interview, this one. I have already been up to Peterborough and am coming through London on the way down to Kent. 'Have you eaten?' my host greets me, sensing immediately that I have not. 'Come through to the kitchen and I'll make something.' Katie Boyle is someone who notices things, and after years of training as a newspaper agony aunt, she has listened to more personal problems than most would care to contemplate. You can see why people like to talk to her and write to her. Even talking about death, there is calm reassurance in her voice.

'I've been aware of death being part of life ever since I was a very young child. My stepmother died in my arms when I was fourteen, and it was the most agonizing, amputating experience I could possibly have had. I adored her. Then there were a sequence of friends; then my father died; then I was widowed. I have always had a tremendous belief in there being something further than this life, so I am attracted to anything that makes me feel comforted.'

The stanza she has chosen shows death as the most seamless passage from one state to another. But does it idealize dying?

'No. It takes into consideration the fact we are both body and soul, and therefore we need imagery because we are hemmed in by the need to use the physical dimensions. I hear, touch and feel, so what better in the basic and elementary conditions we live in in this world, than imagery that will give both the feeling of hope and that we understand exactly what might happen. I am not saying it will happen, but I like the imagery it conjures up.'

'If the image is of a voyage,' I ask, 'what is at the furthest point?'

'I am taught, as a Catholic, that we are all going to go through a certain stage of purgatory, and therefore if I am in pain, or if I want something terribly badly, I'll offer that prayer for a soul in purgatory so I stay there a little less time. I still do it, and I feel that there is a very understanding God. I believe that we will have peace and happiness and be surrounded by all the things that we really like. I can't imagine going over there and not being met by my long-gone dogs, cats and other pets. I am sure I will see the most beautiful flowers, views, trees and everyone I really want to meet. Okay, you think I romanticize it, but I don't think I do! We have all been through our hell in one way or another in this world, and I like to think that what we call heaven is complete contentment.'

Katie Boyle is a former fashion model, four-times host of the Eurovision Song Contest, *and of numerous radio series, including* Katie and Friends *for Radio 2. For twenty years, she answered emotional and practical questions of every kind in her 'Dear Katie' column in the* TV Times. *More recently, she became the agony aunt for dog owners, writing in the magazine* Dogs Today.

What is dying?
I am standing on the sea shore,
a ship sails to the morning breeze
and starts for the ocean.
She is an object of beauty
and I stand watching her
till at last she fades
on the horizon
and someone at my side says
'She is gone'.
Gone! Where?
Gone from my sight – that is all.
She is just as large in the masts, hull and spars
as she was when I saw her,
and just as able to bear her load of living
freight to its destination.
The diminished size and total loss of sight is in me,
not in her;
and just at the moment when someone at my side says,
'She is gone'
there are others who are watching her coming,
and other voices take up a glad shout –
'There she comes!'
– and that is dying.

'The Ship' by Bishop Brent (1862–1929)

Melvyn Bragg

'As a set of words, it has to do with religion, revelation and understanding – why and wherefore, the meaning and the purpose. But the words apply to everything we think about. They can lighten our darkness about areas of knowledge, or about the relationships we have with people. Generally we move forward in a fog. We have this one life and we stumble through it. We look back and see certain clear lines, most of them going in wrong directions, but the idea of getting some light on the way we are going, and why we are going (whether it is in work or in any aspect of our lives) seems to me profoundly important and much yearned for by everyone – unless they have developed an ignorant cynicism.'

Melvyn Bragg is a wordsmith. Each of his roles – novelist, journalist, broadcaster, playwright – makes different demands on the spoken and written word. The Prayer Book collects, as models of tightly-wrought language, are exemplary, and allow a width and depth of interpretation. The well-known collect from Evening Prayer, for aid against all perils, contains the line 'defend us from all perils and dangers of this night'. Is this bodyguard protection?

'I don't think of it as a bodyguard. I think it is a hope. There has to be something else, which continues, takes us forward and takes us into another time. I feel that so strongly. And yet we have no final proof of it, unless we absolutely believe in the resurrection; which takes us to the line of the prayer which brings in the question of faith and belief: "for the love of thy only Son, our Saviour Jesus Christ". That is an act of faith, and faith is probably the most complicated thing of all, because it is inexplicable and yet inescapable. Many people do not know what it means, but they know that it is there; and the idea of faith, and the reaching out for it, is very strong. So this clear and magnificent prayer speaks both to people who are inside the church, and to people who have – or are trying to rediscover, as I am in a rather solitary, very fragile and tentative way – a faith. It speaks to them, and it speaks to people who feel, as I did until quite recently, that it is nothing to do with any formal faiths, and who still think about life and the way

20

it is being led. It speaks to all of these, in three different lines which I would describe as a real prayer (the first line), a hope (the second), and a question of faith (the third). And the one leads to the other one way, yet if you read them in reverse order, they still make sense.'

Melvyn Bragg is one of the major figures in the world of the arts. A writer of plays, screenplays, and novels, he was appointed Controller of Arts, London Weekend Television, in 1990.

Lighten our darkness, we beseech thee, O Lord;
and by thy great mercy defend us from all perils
   and dangers of this night;
for the love of thy only Son, our Saviour, Jesus Christ.
Amen.

Book of Common Prayer (1662)

Adrian Cadbury

The Cadburys have a long history of doing things. John, a Quaker who was born in 1801, founded the cocoa and chocolate business which has become something of a household name. After his son George took it over, he moved the factory and founded a village for the workers, Bournville, which became a prototype for modern housing and planning methods. Getting things done is a passion for their descendants too. Sir Adrian Cadbury points to a passage in the Epistle of St James which he finds an inspiration.

'Many of the injunctions one reads are about what *not* to do, and it worries me that that can be rather a negative approach. What I like about this passage is that it is extremely positive. You have got to get out there and do something.

'The second reason I like it is that I regard the advice in this passage as a letter being sent to friends who will keep it by them, and, when in need of encouragement and advice, will turn to it. The advice is essentially practical, so we have got something that is positive, practical, and which you can go back to when you are in doubt.

'The bit about the hearing is important. You have to listen as well. But having listened, you then have to act. To me, one cannot just wring one's hands about the state of the world, but you try to do something about it, however modest. One may feel that anything an individual can do is not really going to make much difference. But in fact it is only if each of us, as individuals, does something, however small, that we will get things moving in the right direction.'

This is the moment to introduce the strange image – described by St James – of a man looking in a mirror, going away, and immediately forgetting what he looks like. Is this an allusion to the common condition of self-deception?

'It is a very graphic illustration. You look at yourself in the mirror, recognize yourself for what you are, and then you move on and you do not take to heart the lesson of that self-examination. The difficulty, partly, is that there are always pressing matters that need to be attended to. We know in our hearts that there are some (perhaps) major changes that we ought to make in our way of life, but there are so many other things which have to be done right away, that they take over. So this brief period of self-realization passes away and it is difficult to act on it.'

I ask how to avoid that deafness which hears but instantly forgets.

'The way to do it is to have in mind, like looking in the mirror, what you believe you stand for and must live up to. That gives the goal, and you try not to lose sight of it.'

'And after that?'

'And then you have to do it!'

Sir Adrian Cadbury, a former chairman of Cadbury Schweppes, was a director of the Bank of England from 1970 to 1994.

Be ye doers of the word,
and not hearers only, deceiving your own selves.
For if any be a hearer of the word, and not a doer,
he is like unto a man beholding his natural face
    in a glass:
For he beholdeth himself,
and goeth his way,
and straightway forgetteth what manner of man
    he was.

James 1.22–24
(Authorized Version)

Clive Calver

The general director of the Evangelical Alliance can claim to represent more than a million Christians from more than twenty denominations. Clive Calver is also a founder of the massive Christian festival, Spring Harvest, and programme director of Mission England. In other words, he thinks big. In that context it seems fitting to be discussing the contents of a prayer used by General Lord Astley before the battle of Edge Hill.

'We all have our pet tyrannies – the things that really hassle us – and for me it is the busy-ness of life, and the variety of calls that can be made on you which come from the variety of people's needs. It is possible, when you have been dashing from pillar to post, to push the Lord into the background, however little you want to do that.'

I decide to deal first with the most obvious, if slightly suspicious, view of it – as something of an opt-out clause. Could it be that?

'Yes, it could. But it also speaks of a spiritual reality. Even when we do get so embroiled in the things of the day that God is pushed to the background, he does not forget us. He is always with us, by his Holy Spirit, for all who have made that personal commitment to him. He is not going to leave them, and that is a tremendous reassurance. We can abuse that, and we can take for granted that he will be there. But, equally, he has made the promise that he will be there, and that is something we can call upon, especially when we get so busy that everything else is intruding and we do not have time.

'You only avoid its becoming an opt-out clause when you realize that God's spirit does not always strive with someone and that if the Lord is continually nudging and reminding and challenging, then you need to listen. That obedience is part of the Christian life, and you cannot presume upon the grace of God even though he is always there. You want him to look at you as a good and faithful servant, not as a rebellious self-willed son who refuses to do what he is supposed to be doing.

'I think that prayer is a conscious expression of love and

commitment to God. When I am talking to my wife, those are very special moments; the same applies when I am talking to my children. But even when I am not talking to them the relationship is still there. This prayer is an acknowledgement of that. Lord, it says, if we do not have time for an adequate conversation in the next few hours, please hang on to me and I am certainly hanging on to you.

'Being with God is the one divine continuum. As David says in the Psalms, "where can I go from your presence, how can I ever get away from it, Lord?" The answer is, you can't. Therefore everything we do is done in God's presence, and everything we do not do is time spent in God's presence. A number of friends have said as they have approached the end of their lives, that if they had one thing they would change, they would do less and pray more. I am beginning to feel that same way too.'

The Revd Clive Calver, now president of the World Relief Corporation, was director general of the Evangelical Alliance from 1983 to 1997.

O Lord,
thou knowest how busy I must be this day;
if I forget thee,
do not thou forget me.

General Lord Astley (1579–1652)
before the battle of Edge Hill

John Cole

It was Saint Augustine who wrote the famous line 'Our hearts are restless till they find their rest in thee'. The BBC's former political editor, John Cole, describes Augustine's line as a springboard for his own choice of prayer, a verse from a poem by George Herbert. The poem links the consequence of restlessness to the weariness which pervades the human condition.

'Weariness is a spiritual vacuum and many of us are in danger of constantly slipping into a spiritual vacuum because our spiritual life gets crowded out by something that appears more interesting. Restlessness comes in periods when everything is going perfectly well in the rest of my life. So well, in fact, that I fill every hour and, too often, every minute, and do not get enough time to sleep, think, read or pray. It is a sense of being overburdened with the things of the world.

'Weariness can come from many things. Sadly, for many people it comes through illness. I have had my share of that, although not excessively so. But the weariness I am talking about is not that. It is the weariness of day-to-day life, of driving yourself, doing the things that you want to do in your professional, personal and family life, and just leaving no corner for your own intellectual and spiritual nourishment. When we are considering the rich young ruler in the New Testament, I always think that his problem probably was not simply wealth, but that he had a rich life. It is too easy to allow the spiritual side of life to get crowded out, and I assume that that is what the story of the rich young ruler was about. This prayer bears on that, because the burden of happiness – richness in the wider sense – was too great for him. The poem says that only weariness of *that* will, perhaps, attract that sort of man to God.

'If you define weariness as a kind of a spiritual vacuum which you feel an urge to fill, then I think it *is* weariness that pushes many people to do the things that are necessary to get themselves into the spirit of God's universe. That is to read, think and pray.'

'Is that what you do yourself?'

'Yes it is, but not often enough. That is why I like this

prayer, which expresses the kind of longing for a more ful-filled spiritual life to match my well-fulfilled professional and family life.'

John Cole was the BBC's Political Editor, 1982–92.

Yet let him keep the rest,
But keep them with repining restlessness;
Let him be rich and weary, that at least,
If goodness lead him not, yet weariness
May toss him to my breast.

George Herbert (1593–1633)
from 'The Pulley'

Stephanie Cole

'For me, one the most difficult things about belief is the doubt.'
The actress, known to many as the lovably disagreeable Diana
from the television comedy *Waiting for God* has put her finger
on one of the most pressing concerns of religion. Face to face,
she delivers it with considerably more serenity than her television character would ever allow.

'Doubting distresses me terribly, so whenever I am in periods
of great doubt, I go to this passage from St John. He speaks
very succinctly to those of us who have doubt in whatever
belief system we live our lives. I think he speaks for all people,
of all time, in all belief systems, and that is one of the things
that I love about it.'

Many other people love it too. The passage is full of the
most quotable quotes. We ponder one of them: 'In my Father's
house are many mansions'.

'I think there is a mansion there for everybody. I take it that
there are as many paths to God as there are people in this
world. God goes under any number of names, and there is a
place for everybody. Of course there is! How could there not
be? Of course I have terrible moments of doubt, which is why
the phrase "Let not your heart be troubled" is a huge moment
for me, when I breathe and I think, "Now, just let go of the
doubt, listen to that and think. Just go into that place which is
silent and peaceful inside me, and know that that is how it is."'

I suggest to her that, since Thomas, one of the disciples,
found Jesus' words confusing, she might be excused for doing
so too.

'That is interesting you should say it is confusing. I take it
that Thomas is saying, "Look, you're telling us all this but I
can't believe it. How can I be sure?" and Jesus is saying, "Look,
if it were not so, I would have told you. I am going before you
to prepare a place for you." What he is trying to do is reassure
by saying, "Listen to me, Thomas. Just listen to me, quietly
and calmly. Stop panicking and just listen." And all the time
Thomas . . .'

She breaks off for a moment to apply her acting skills to the
answer.

'If I were playing this scene as Thomas, I would be there in a terrible state saying, "But you're going and I don't believe, and you've told us all these things but I can't touch it, I can't believe it. I mean, how can I know?" and Jesus is saying, "It's okay, it's okay – I'm gonna be there and it's gonna be fine." That's how I take it. There is somebody calming someone down. Just take a breath and you'll know that it is okay.'

Stephanie Cole plays Diana in the television comedy Waiting for God. *She played in* Open All Hours *and performed one of Alan Bennett's 'Talking Heads' monologues.*

Let not your heart be troubled;
ye believe in God; believe also in me.
In my Father's house are many mansions:
if it were not so, I would have told you.
I go to prepare a place for you.
And if I go and prepare a place for you, I will come
    again and receive you unto myself;
that where I am, there ye may be also.
And whither I go ye know, and the way ye know.
Thomas saith unto him,
Lord, we know not whither thou goest, and how can
    we know the way?
Jesus saith unto him,
I am the way, the truth, and the life:
no man cometh unto the Father, but by me.
If ye had known me, ye should have known my
    Father also:
and from henceforth ye know him,
and have seen him.

John 14.1–7
(Authorized Version)

Margaret Court

The stage is set for the final of the 100th Ladies Tennis Championships at Wimbledon. It is a time to flick back through the record books. There, in the historic roll of champions, is the name of Margaret Court, singles winner not once but three times. With her sixty-four grand slam titles, many would say she is the greatest ladies player of all time. Yet, to her, it all seems strangely remote.

'It is not until I come back to Wimbledon that I look and I think, Did I ever really play here? Did I win all that? It is a part of my life that seems so far away because I became a Christian when I was still at the top in tennis in 1972. I always knew my talent and my gift was from God, but I knew that there was something still missing in my life. You can hold that Wimbledon trophy up above your head, and can have all that, but still have nothing. And it was not until I accepted Jesus that I had that reality, and I look back and think, Did I ever really play?'

Paul is assuring his fellow believers in Ephesus of his prayers for them, and he gives a long list of spiritual gifts – wisdom, revelation and enlightenment are among them. But could these terms become mere Christian jargon?

'It says in the Scriptures that you will never understand them until you become spiritually alive to them, and give your heart to Jesus Christ. When we believe in our hearts, and confess with our mouths, that Jesus is Lord, it says in the Scriptures, we shall be saved. When you do that, the most wonderful miracle happens on the inside, the spiritual-man is recreated. And when that happens in your life then you can take this wonderful prayer and start praying, "Father, give it to me richly in all wisdom and knowledge, and spiritual understanding, that, the eyes of my understanding being enlightened, I may know the hope of your calling." We can pray that prayer in our own life, and the word becomes real. I know that in my own life I have had tremendous healing through the Scriptures by taking God's word as medicine. I had a torn valve of the heart and through sitting under God's word and meditating it, thinking, eating and sleeping it – just like natural food is to our own body – my heart was totally healed through the Scriptures. So I know how powerful they are and we can take God's word as medicine in our own lives and our outer-man will get in line with our spiritual-man.'

I ask about Paul's references to 'the hope of his calling' and 'the riches of the glory of his inheritance in the saints'.

'When you know Jesus Christ as Lord, you are already seated in heavenly places by faith. So often we have said "Our Father, let it be here on earth as it is in heaven", and I believe that the Lord wants us to know him here on earth as it is in heaven. Then we can walk in divine health, in the peace of God, knowing the reality of Jesus, his authority and love in everyday life. Paul's prayer is encouraging Christians that that walk can be made here on earth. We don't have to wait until we go to heaven.'

Margaret Court holds more tennis championship titles than any other player in history: Australian Champion 1960–66, 1969–71, 1973; French Champion 1962, 1964, 1969–70, 1973; Wimbledon Champion 1963, 1965, 1970; USA Champion 1962, 1965, 1969–70, 1973.

I cease not to give thanks for you, making mention of
  you in my prayers;
That the God of our Lord Jesus Christ, the Father of
  glory,
may give unto you the spirit of wisdom and revelation
  in the knowledge of him:
The eyes of your understanding being enlightened;
that ye may know what is the hope of his calling,
what the riches of the glory of his inheritance in the
  saints,
and what is exceeding greatness of his power to
  us-ward who believe,
according to the working of his mighty power,
  which he wrought in Christ,
when he raised him from the dead,
and set him at his own right hand in the heavenly
  places.

Ephesians 1.16–20
(Authorized Version)

Wendy Craig

'I had gone through a time of anxiety after my husband died when I thought I was not going to be able to cope with everything I suddenly had to do. I thought that, without him, I was going to go under, and not manage, and I got more and more anxious. I was reading the work of St Augustine one day, came across this little prayer, and realized that there was a great deal of truth in it. It really spoke to me, and I have prayed it many times since.'

I ask her what she understands by the sentence 'Do not be afraid to throw yourself on the Lord'.

'To me it means abandoning yourself totally to his love. If you want to cry, then cry. If you want to shout, shout. Just abandon yourself to him.'

'Is that what you do?'

'I do! Yes.' She chuckles. 'You should hear me walking my dog through the fields. I sometimes have a really good shout! On the other hand I often sing praises very loudly too! Some people are afraid to do that in case they don't get a response. They think, supposing I do that and nothing happens. Or some people might be very strong and get embarrassed at the thought of doing it. But you should never be too proud to do it.'

So to the line 'He will not draw back and let you fall'. Is that a cushion?

'I would not call it a cushion. I would call it a helping hand. He does not mean you have got to stop doing everything. He means he will help you. When you pray a prayer with all your heart, the Holy Spirit will come into you and give you a feeling of calm and support. I just gave him a great list of things one day and said, Look, all these letters to be answered, I have got to do personal appearances here, there and everywhere. I cannot do it on my own, can you please help me? And as soon as I had said that to him I felt much calmer. The Lord used other people to help me in a practical way, and help did come.'

Wendy Craig is an actress known for her roles in Nanny *and* Butterflies *to name but two. She won major acting awards in the '60s, '70s and '80s, and has a gold disc to her credit as well.*

Do not be afraid to throw yourself on the Lord;
He will not draw back and let you fall.
Put your worries aside and throw yourself on him.
He will welcome you and heal you.

St Augustine (354–430)

Dana

'Sometimes you will come across a prayer which really touches something within you. You think, oh that's very comforting, or truthful, and it just sheds light on something.'

The prayer is part of a hymn by James Quinn. It takes the image of a vine tree with the Son of God represented by the tree itself and each individual as a branch. The Father is the one who tends the tree, cutting away the branches which have no fruit, and pruning those which do. In her gentle, Irish lilt, the singer explains the image.

'Learning about myself is very difficult. There are areas of my character that need working on. You find you keep making the same mistakes, and doing the same stupid things. I can feel I am not getting anywhere or that I am really failing. And then I read this. And what it says is, you are not failing but learning. You are being pruned so that you can be lively, useful and fruit-bearing to other people.'

'What fruit do you hope to bear?'

'I think we are all called to be Christ in the world and to bring his love, so that when people meet us, their lives are better for the meeting. They should feel, through us, a sense of being loved. There is such a lack of love in the world. It causes such pain, rejection and terrible hurt in people's lives.'

I ask about the image of God as the gardener, carefully pruning branches. Has she ever felt that something has been carefully cut back in order to release new life?

'That is one of the things I have been learning. I used to get very distressed, and would think, I am not getting anywhere and might as well give up. But to see this insight – that out of love he carefully prunes us – is very freeing. The areas that they work on are those of the little burdens we carry: we have an automatic reaction and we don't know why; someone says something that suddenly hurts very deeply and we don't know why it hurts. And then it is as though he is weeding out. Through prayer, he begins to show me what the root cause is. It is a pruning but it is very freeing. It is like letting go of another hurt that is inside you, which does become filled with a sense of love, and that you are really cared for.'

Dana is the singer who at the age of nineteen won the 1970 Eurovision Song Contest with the song 'All Kinds of Everything'. It went on to reach number one in many countries including Ireland, South Africa, Australia and the UK. Since then there have been many other chart successes, though more recently her career has moved into pantomime, acting and television.

I am the holy vine,
Which God my Father tends.
Each branch that yields no fruit
My Father cuts away.
Each fruitful branch
He prunes with care
To make it yield
Abundant fruit.

I am the fruitful vine,
And you my branches are.
He who abides in me
I will in him abide.
So shall ye yield
Much fruit, but none
If you remain
Apart from me.

James Quinn (b. 1919)

Ken Dodd

'When I say my prayers, I say the Lord's Prayer and quite a lot of others – "I want . . ." and "will you do . . .", and "will it be possible . . ." and "could I have . . .". Oh, and I do remember to say "thank you" and "praise God" and "thank you for my life". But at the very end I like to say: May the grace of our Lord Jesus Christ, and the love of God, and the fellowship of the Holy Spirit, be with us all now, and for evermore. Amen. I say it because it means someone else is there with you. I think a lot of people – well I do anyway – feel that we are all very much alone. But we are assured by Jesus Christ that we are not alone. He is with us always and it is very comforting. It certainly means a lot to me to know that I have someone with me all the time.

'I think it does reaffirm the faith that has been passed on. You were instructed as a child to believe in the Trinity, and the grace and love of God. The love of God is very important. If he loves me, well, perhaps I am not such a bad fellow after all. And the fellowship of the Holy Spirit suggests a sort of a guardian angel with you all the time. We all have times of sorrow and sadness when, maybe, your faith slips a little bit. But then, all of a sudden, you feel a tremendous feeling of courage and confidence, and that is this prayer. They are with you all the time.'

The words of the grace are so frequently heard that there is always a danger of their meaning getting lost. I ask how that is to be prevented, and, from his chuckle, take it that I have asked the right person.

'Now this is something I can understand. I am quite an expert on this. You see, I am a comedian and I tell jokes. Very often I tell the same jokes night after night after night, rather like an actor repeats the same lines every night. But you never do them the same. You never ever do a joke the same way. I have been a professional comedian now since 1954 – it is a long time ago – and in all that time, I tell everybody, I have never ever done the same show twice. But they never lose their meaning – it's the way you tell it! As the man says, it's the way he tells them! Your intonation, the amount of drive and of

your own persona you put behind the line, makes the joke
fresh every time. The joke comes fresh, the lines of an actor
come up fresh every time, and the lines of a prayer can come
up fresh every time. Sometimes an emphasis on one word,
sometimes on the other, sometimes an underlining – but it
does come up fresh every time.'

*Ken Dodd is a comedian, an entertainer, actor, singer
and a man who once set a new record at the London
Palladium with his own forty-two-week season. His
famous diddy men and tickling sticks have taken their
place in folk culture.*

> May the grace of our Lord Jesus Christ,
> and the love of God,
> and the fellowship of the Holy Spirit,
> be with us all
> now,
> and for evermore.
> Amen.

From 2 Corinthians 13.14

Alice Thomas Ellis

The ancient Latin hymn *Salve Regina* has inspired generations of musicians and artists as they have worked over and further embellished the well-loved lines. It has also been an inspiration to the writer Alice Thomas Ellis, she says. I ask her why. She begins to tell me, then pauses a while, trying to weigh up whether it would be better to say no more. Slowly, she concedes.

'I've always found Our Lady an enormous source of comfort. I get very tired of people these days denigrating her as the handmaiden of the Lord. They say that is too humble. But I like the prayer because it gives her the proper respect and admits her true dignity.

'In my very worst time, I remembered that Our Lady stood at the foot of the cross. But she did not fling herself about, tearing her hair and weeping. She was just enormously brave and staunch and accepting. When our son died, he had been in a coma for eleven months beforehand. I think if I had not believed in God I could not have borne it. I also felt that wherever he had gone, there would be someone to look after him that would be not merely a father, but also a mother to make sure that he was all right.'

'Did you pray to Mary at that time?'

'I think I talked to her in my mind nearly all of the time.'

The *Salve Regina* shows raw feeling. It talks of 'our sighs, mourning and weeping in this vale of tears'. I ask whether those feelings ever dominate within her?

'They certainly do. I just cannot go along with the pretence that everything here is fine and getting better. It seems to me to be getting worse and worse all the time. I see no evidence of progress or any grounds for temporal hope. I believe in the first words of the old catechism – Who made you? God made me. Why did he make you? To love and obey him in this world and be happy with him for ever in the next. I have given up looking for real temporal happiness or satisfaction, and I think if you spend your life looking for happiness you are going to be very disappointed. I think it is a side issue. If you are happy then you are very fortunate, but I certainly do not think you gain anything by the pursuit of happiness.

'The plea for grace and mercy is the most hopeful high point of the prayer. There is light at the end of the tunnel that is not the light of an oncoming train. There is hope. We are promised joy, but I do not think we should expect it now.'

Alice Thomas Ellis is a writer and novelist. Books include Unexplained Laughter *(Yorkshire Post Novel of the Year, 1985), and* The Inn at the Edge of the World *(Writers' Guild Award, 1990).*

Hail, holy Queen,
Mother of mercy;
hail our life, our sweetness and our hope.
To thee do we cry, poor banished children of Eve;
to thee do we send up our sighs, mourning and
    weeping in this vale of tears.
Turn, then, most gracious advocate, thine eyes
    of mercy towards us;
and after this our exile, show unto us the blessed
    fruit of thy womb, Jesus.
O clement,
O loving,
O sweet Virgin Mary.

Ranulph Fiennes

The world's greatest living explorer, they call him. Ranulph Fiennes has led no fewer than ten major expeditions, including an extraordinary journey across the Antarctic continent, via the South Pole. My first impression is that he is not one to indulge in idle chit-chat. I ask him why he likes the Lord's Prayer, and he tells me straight.

'It's a good bit of very practical prose, and does not fall under the heavy, wordy sort of verbiage of quite a lot of stuff in the Prayer Book. It is really handy, small, neat, easily remembered and very apt.'

Its substance is timeless and on a massive scale. So is the prayer a statement of general aspiration, or one for individual circumstances?

'It is a bit of both. Because I was brought up on it, it has become a homely thing, and in strange places that is comforting. Second, it is a help in that I do not like to ask for help, even though there is an apparent need for it in some hostile parts of the world that we travel through. It seems wrong to be asking for help, so I perhaps cheat by subconsciously wanting help but, by saying the Lord's Prayer, thinking about other people as well. When you are running short of rations, for example, a very useful bit would be "Give us this day our daily bread". But on the last trip I made the habit of thinking about the people in Sarajevo and in Ethiopia at that point, rather than our own dwindling rations.'

'What do you mean by comfort in strange places?'

'Places like Antarctica and the Arctic Ocean and the big deserts – I mean hot deserts – are strange. The stranger you feel, the more natural it is to start thinking about the person who made all these strange things, the Creator.'

I ask about the last two lines of the prayer.

'"Lead us not into temptation". That is talking about all sorts of things which you can do wrong, but you could stop yourself. "Deliver us from evil" refers to those things which are quite beyond our own capabilities. So I am thinking about temptation being something which I can personally either stop myself getting into or fall for. When it comes to evil, it is

40

helpful to be able to say to yourself that, maybe these things of which you find yourself being frightened, are more powerful than you, but not more powerful than your particular ally – which is God. In my case, since God is difficult to imagine, it is Jesus Christ who I am actually praying to. Then in the darkness of the tent, you are doing the act of crossing yourself to remind you that he, as a person, sat with apprehension, knowing that some nasty blokes are going to come and stick him on a cross, which is about the nastiest sort of three-day death you can think of. He managed to put up with that, and still go ahead with it. So if he can do that, then obviously it makes it much easier to realize that you can do a lot more than you think.'

Sir Ranulph Fiennes is an explorer who led the longest polar journey in history (1,345 miles).

Our Father which art in heaven,
Hallowed be thy Name,
Thy kingdom come,
Thy will be done,
In earth as it is in heaven.
Give us this day our daily bread;
And forgive us our trespasses,
As we forgive them that trespass against us;
And lead us not into temptation,
But deliver us from evil.
Amen.

Book of Common Prayer (1662)

Douglas Gresham

Little Douglas is one of the key players in the story of C. S. Lewis and his love for the dying American woman Joy Gresham, who became his wife. It is a story which touches hearts each time it is told, from Lewis' own account, to the play *Shadowlands* and more recently the film. Douglas is not so little now. Having known him through his very public childhood, it is especially interesting to meet the man.

'The whole of my Christian behavioural patterns are based on this passage of Scripture,' he begins, turning to a passage from Paul's letter to the Galatians.

'It is about the difference between following Christ in the Spirit – leaving your sinful nature on the cross with him – and gratifying the sinful nature quite deliberately.'

Paul's advice is to live by the Spirit. But how does he recognize what is of the Spirit?

'There are two ways. The first is to read what Galatians says about it, and that is fairly categorical. But it is also by the results of one's planned actions, or by the planned results of one's actions, that one can recognize what is the Spirit. Anything that will be to the detriment of, or cause pain or hurt to another human being, or even another of God's creatures is not of the Spirit.'

'How do you then live by it?'

'That is a very much more difficult thing to do. Being a Christian is an expensive procedure. It costs in terms of personal comfort, financial commitments, and far more, in my case, in terms of time. Each of us has only a finite time on this planet, and that can be spent in the pursuit of one's own enjoyment, or in the pursuit of serving Christ. To be a Christian, and to pursue the life of the Spirit, involves the giving back of that time to Christ.'

I move on to the part in which Paul warns against gratifying the desires of the sinful nature. Is life by the Spirit, I wonder, about suppressing a part of your own nature?

'Initially, yes. One of my problems throughout life has been a very high sexual libido, and I have had to give that to Christ, I have had to sacrifice that on the cross – to kill that on the cross with Jesus. And that has meant that for a long time I have had to fight those sexual desires, and those desires to gratify the sinful nature. But another thing the Scripture tells us is that if you *do* defy Satan and his temptations, he will flee from you, and those sorts of things have been helped so enormously over the past years by following the Spirit as much as possible. It is not something that is easy to do, and I don't think it is possible to live entirely by the Spirit; one has to continue to strive to do so. But, yes, I have suffered crushing depressions in the past, and they have been lifted over the years. Anxieties and fears – all of those sorts of difficulties in my life – have been much alleviated. I won't say they have been cured, but they have been much alleviated from following what Paul has said, and giving my life to Christ.'

Douglas Gresham is the son of Joy Gresham, who married C. S. Lewis.

Live by the Spirit, and you will not gratify the
    desires of the sinful nature.
For the sinful nature desires what is contrary
    to the Spirit,
and the Spirit what is contrary to the sinful nature.
They are in conflict with each other, so that you
    do not do what you want.
But if you are led by the Spirit, you are not under law.
The acts of the sinful nature are obvious:
sexual immorality, impurity and debauchery;
idolatry and witchcraft;
hatred, discord, jealously, fits of rage, selfish ambition,
    dissensions, factions and envy;
drunkenness, orgies, and the like.
I warn you, as I did before,
that those who live like this will not inherit the
    kingdom of God.
But the fruit of the Spirit is love, joy, peace, patience,
    kindness, goodness, faithfulness, gentleness
    and self-control.
Against such things there is no law.

Galatians 5.16–23
(New International Version)

Edward Heath

Words can acquire power through association. A simple catch-phrase can bring to mind a whole personality in a flash. At other times, though, it is an occasion which is remembered. The prayer Sir Edward has chosen takes him back to an international gathering he was called to attend soon after becoming Prime Minister, to celebrate the 25th anniversary of the United Nations.

'It was an inspiration – that whatever happened one should press ahead. No matter how critical the press is, how hostile your opponents are, how unappreciative the country seems to be, or how horrible the world is becoming, this should not be abandoned. That was why it appealed to me, and I think that is why it made an impact on the United Nations. You carry on and see it through to the end.'

I ask what comes within Drake's term the 'great matter'.

'For me it is to try to bring about a fuller life for my fellow citizens, in which they can have a better understanding of philosophy and religion and all the other basic aspects of life, quite apart from the material benefits which they are also entitled to enjoy. Since the end of the Second World War this has been dominated by a determination to prevent Europe ever tearing itself apart again. My generation passed through the war, and those who survived wanted to bring this about. We have seen Europe torn apart for centuries, and we are determined to prevent this ever happening again. That is why the "great matter" was to bring about a united Europe. Now we have got a united Europe, and our task must be to make it more effective for those purposes.'

I turn to the line 'it is not the beginning but the continuing of the same until it is thoroughly finished which yieldeth the true glory'. What of those things which are so great that they cannot lie within the scope of one individual or one lifetime?

'That part of the prayer is very necessary because, so often when you have been struggling hard, you say, Is this really worth it – or, I had better pack it in. That can never achieve the results which you set out to get, and should therefore never be contemplated. If you have got something which is beyond the means of a single individual's *métier* then the art lies in persuading others to support you in what you are doing. And the further stage, if you cannot carry it through in your own lifetime, is in persuading other people to continue it after you have had to give it up.'

The prayer refers to the example of Christ, 'who for the finishing of thy work, lay down his life for us'. What in that example does the former Prime Minister seek to follow?

'I would seek to follow the example of his lifetime. The crucifixion was not something he brought about himself. It was forced upon him by other people. But in the many aspects of his death, the one which is important is that it meant he lives, both in history and in the Christian belief. So his work carries on because of the fact that he was brought to his death.'

Sir Edward Heath was Prime Minister from 1970 until 1974. Since leaving the front benches he has remained in the forefront of British politics, especially on European issues.

O Lord God,
when thou givest to thy servants to endeavour
any great matter;
grant us also to know that
it is not the beginning but the continuing of the
    same until it is thoroughly finished
which yieldeth the true glory.
Through him who, for the finishing of thy work,
lay down his life for us, our redeemer, Jesus Christ.

Based on a saying of Sir Francis Drake

45

Larry Hollingworth

'Oh, he's seen more than anyone.' The BBC news correspondent roundly endorses the former chief of operations for the UNHCR. 'If anyone has seen it,' he tells me, 'Larry has.' Throughout the cruel and shocking war in Bosnia and the surrounding Balkan countries, the Father Christmas-like figure, with his distinctively large white beard, answered television reporters' questioning on horrifying events with extraordinary patience and calm. When I meet him, he is busy trying to get a flight back to the war zone. Dangerous it may be, but Larry Hollingworth is a man for today rather than tomorrow. His choice of prayer reflects that exactly.

'It is a prayer that has been a favourite for so many years, and it became a favourite without my realizing it. In fact, I used to say it regularly without realizing it was a prayer. It is simple, short, and rhymes, and these few words encapsulate my thoughts.'

I ask him whether the idea, to make the point, has been overstated. To my surprise he says not.

'For me, it is genuine. Obviously, I am not suggesting to people that they go away and burn their life insurance policies, or that they should not top-up the pension fund. What I am saying is that today, now, is the most important time of your life, and if you can be helped through now, you will make tomorrow.'

'Isn't it sometimes irresponsible not to worry about things?'

'I don't think it is irresponsible just to think about today. Sometimes it can be irresponsible to be obsessed with tomorrow, and not to live happily today. People think, Ah, it's going to be great when I have retired, I am going to own a yacht, or, I am going to go on a sea cruise, and everything is geared to tomorrow. I believe this prayer tells me, enjoy *now*. Enjoy, as you are working, breathing and looking.'

My mind turns back to those reports from Bosnia, where he has spent so many months. It is one thing when times are good. What about those people for whom today is misery, and for whom tomorrow is their only source of hope?

'Six or seven weeks ago I was in the Krajna in Bosnia and I

watched almost 200,000 people who were driven out of the Krajna with their tractors and with their possessions. Only two or three days beforehand, they had been tilling the land in the homes which they had owned for 500 years. Here they were on this road going off to know-not-where. They had no idea where they were going or what they were going to do when they got there. Some I spoke to simply cried and sobbed; some blamed the Croats, others blamed the Muslims. But some were quite calm, and said, "It has happened and it is done. We now have to move on and we have to see what happens." And they were happy that the four wheels on the tractor were still turning, or that the towing-hook was still pulling the trailer, or that the few possessions they had were still there. It was a sunny and a happy day. That was not irresponsibility on their behalf. They were accepting and making the best of the situation of that particular day.'

Larry Hollingworth worked for the UN High Commission for Refugees during the long war in the former Yugoslavia. He became famous for the guts and diplomacy with which he brought supplies to Bosnian towns under siege.

Lord, for tomorrow and its need I do not pray:
Keep me, O Lord, just for today.

Paul Jones

Manfred Mann was in the vanguard of the 1960s' pop revolution. The group's lead singer later turned to acting, but Paul Jones still kept the gold albums coming, with the original recording of *Evita*, to name but one. Curiously, he is one of two singers – from entirely different traditions – who chose the same passage from St Paul's letter to the Philippians. The tenor Robert Tear spoke to me about it a year or two later. They selected different translations, and offered very different personal understandings of St Paul's words.

'One thinks of Christian joy in the word "Rejoice". It is not about mindlessly grinning your way through the day, but rather a deep understanding that we have eternal life, and that the problems and tribulations that we face are temporary. Gentleness, I think, is probably a product of that deep knowledge.

'I see the whole passage, full of commands, as a new year's resolution. I think the command "Do not be anxious" is a very serious one. It is not saying "don't worry about things". It is saying what Jesus said himself: "do not be anxious, but believe".'

But how, by not being anxious about things, do you avoid not being concerned about them?

'I don't think the two things are exclusive at all. I think one has to be *concerned* about things. One has to be seriously concerned about one's own sin and one's own failure to do right every day. That is not the same thing as being anxious about it.'

St Paul's practical advice to keep your mind only on 'whatever is true, noble, right, pure, lovely, admirable, excellent and praiseworthy' raises an equally practical question: how?

'It isn't easy, and for people who regularly read a newspaper or listen to the news on the radio, or watch it on television, it is increasingly difficult. Aided and abetted by the media, we spend most of our time thinking about things that are untrue, impure, ignoble and wrong. I think we have to read our newspaper, and then put it down and say, "I am concerned about those issues, but I am not anxious about them; what I am going to concern my mind about is good things." And the only way to be faced with serious and unpleasant issues and, at the same time, to think about good and noble, and right and pure things, is to pray about those issues. And I don't think Paul is saying "never think about anything else". I think he is saying, "don't let a day go by without thinking about these things".'

Paul Jones launched his career as frontman of the group Manfred Mann, and became one of the highest-selling musicians of the 1960s. He subsequently starred in National Theatre productions, West End shows and television dramas.

Rejoice in the Lord always.
I will say it again: Rejoice!
Let your gentleness be evident to all.
The Lord is near.
Do not be anxious about anything,
but in everything, by prayer and petition,
with thanksgiving,
present your requests to God.
And the peace of God,
which transcends all understanding,
will guard your hearts and your minds in
    Christ Jesus.
Finally, brothers and sisters,
whatever is true,
whatever is noble,
whatever is right,
whatever is pure,
whatever is lovely,
whatever is admirable –
if anything is excellent or praiseworthy –
think about such things.

Philippians 4.4–8
(New International Version)

Diane Louise Jordan

'It is one of the few poems that has lived and grown with me, and as I have changed and developed, the meaning of this poem has had resonances that are relevant to my life right up to today. It is a love poem – probably a love poem in the romantic sense – but after the many readings that I have had of this poem, I realize that it is more than that: it is a poem for me, personally. It is about a greater love.'

Love so often eludes definition. I ask for hers.

'True love only means one thing: opening your arms, embracing and sharing. It is about giving, and, for me, the more you give the more you receive. It is two way – a relationship. Maybe all of us, at some point, have experienced that new feeling of being in love – that almost fantasy love. It is a wild feeling – you just feel tingly and sensational most of the time, and all those little irritable things that can affect you during the day do not matter. Love with God is like that first love, the new romantic love when everything is sparkling and alive. You can feel all the tingles at the tips of your fingers and you know everything is just brilliant.'

'Does your love for God give you a tingle factor as well?'

'Yes,' she laughs, 'I suppose it does!'

The third stanza is still about love, but now about the importance of maintaining a balance between the two halves of the relationship. What is the key?

'Trust.' She pauses, and then adds, 'and always to love in the way that you would like to be loved back. It is so simple. You literally do to others what you would like them to do to you. If you want others to stand by you, and be honest and truthful to you, you have got to practise it too. I have got to love and respect you, as much as you love and respect me. If that happens it cannot die.'

'Have you a love which will never die?'

'I hope so. I pray so. It feels like it at the moment.'

Diane Louise Jordan presented the top children's television programme Blue Peter *for more than six years before moving to* Songs of Praise. *She trained as an actress and has appeared in films and theatre.*

I wonder by my troth, what thou, and I
Did, till we lov'd? were we not wean'd till then?
But suck'd on countrey pleasures, childishly?
Or snorted we in the seaven sleepers den?
T'was so; But this, all pleasures fancies bee.
If ever any beauty I did see,
Which I desir'd, and got, t'was but a dreame of thee.

And now good morrow to our waking soules,
Which watch not one another out of feare;
For love, all love of other sights controules,
And makes one little roome, an every where.
Let sea-discoverers to new worlds have gone,
Let Maps to other, worlds on worlds have showne,
Let us possess one world, each hath one, and is one.

My face in thine eye, thine in mine appeares,
And true plaine hearts doe in the faces rest,
Where we can we finde two better hemispheares
Without sharpe North, without declining West?
What ever dyes, was not mixt equally;
If our two loves be one, or, thou and I
Love so alike, that none doe slacken, none can die.

John Donne (*c.* 1572–1631)
'The Good-Morrow'

Jane Lapotaire

'Real love is about acknowledging that we are all members of the human race, that we are all part of the divine and of the universe. When we see that we are all equally the same, the world will then begin to heal itself.'

Actors and actresses are constantly asked to portray love in one of its many guises. Jane Lapotaire's definition of true love is prompted by the poetic story of an encounter between a hesitant guest (the Unkind, the Ungrateful), and the welcoming host (Love), who is the creator of the guest. How would she respond to such an encounter with this great presence of Love?

'At first I would draw back and be hesitant. But then I would be grateful and blessed, at this presence and dimension of experience – which, after all, is what God is. The divine spark is in each of us, and that love runs through all of us. It is only our egos and our pain that stop us seeing it.'

'Do you – like the guest – try to resist love?'

'I think we all do. We all feel at some time in our lives that we do not deserve love or that we are bad, or that we are riddled with guilt about the way we are as human beings, and we are riddled with shame about that guilt. The world would be a much happier place if we all acknowledged that we are a part of divine love, and that within each human being is a divine spark which is part of the greater whole – call it God or what you will. I think our natural reaction is to draw back and say, But I'm not worthy. You do not have to be worthy. You just have to *be*. So much damage is done in this world today through individuals' lack of self-esteem. So I would invite us all to sit and eat at the table of Love. Love yourself and then you can love other people.'

Jane Lapotaire is an actress who will long be remembered for her title-role performance in Piaf *which won numerous awards including a Broadway Tony. Since then there has been* Shadowlands, *the television series* Love Hurts *and Gertrude opposite Kenneth Branagh in* Hamlet.

Love bade me welcome; yet my soul drew back,
Guilty of dust and sin.
But quick-eyed Love, observing me grow slack
From my first entrance in,
Drew nearer to me, sweetly questioning
If I lack'd anything.

'A guest', I answer'd, 'worthy to be here:'
Love said, 'You shall be she.'*
'I, the Unkind, the Ungrateful? Ah, my dear,
I cannot look on Thee.'
Love took my hand and smiling did reply,
'Who made the eyes but I?'

'Truth, Lord; but I have marr'd them: let my shame
Go where it doth deserve.'
'And know you not,' says Love, 'who bore the blame?'
'My dear, then I will serve.'
'You must sit down,' says Love, 'and taste my meat.'
So I did sit and eat.

George Herbert (1593–1633)

*originally 'he'

Robin Leigh-Pemberton

The sixth-century basilica in Constantinople was built with a vast shallow dome spanning a space never before attempted by human builders. The grandeur of that image, which is our talking-point, matches the grand backdrop of the Governor's room at the Bank of England, as we sit to ponder Edward Gibbon's prose. Gibbon compares the magnificence of the basilica and its dome with the vilest of insects which might be found crawling across it. He seems to make the comparison in favour of the insect.

'It made sense very forcibly – the sense of humility and respect that we ought to have towards God's creation and towards God himself. It is from this position of humility before him that we have the better chance of benefiting from his power, grace and inspiration towards us in dealing with our daily lives. I do not think he is necessarily saying in favour of the insect. What he is reminding us is that the finest achievement of human hands, up to that time, is actually very modest compared with the wonder of the living body, even of the vilest insect that crawls upon the surface of the temple. Here is this little thing that we would think nothing of stepping on, throwing away and despising. Yet it contains within it the marvel of life, the power of procreation and, incidentally, a set of electronic equipment, the like of which no human hand has been able to match. This is the lesson: that we should remain in respect and awe of so many things here on earth, which God has created, and which we take for granted, or which we waste and despise. If we can get that frame of mind clear in our thoughts, then we are on our path to a better relationship with God.

'The most impressive thing in the world is the gift of life and God's spirit working in us. I have found in my life that that is a wonderful source of strength, inspiration and comfort. I do not know whether people will think I have displayed wisdom, but in so far as I have, I believe that it comes from his Holy Spirit, rather than anything from within myself. If you are confronted with great difficulties, under great pressure – and perhaps you will have seen what has happened to me every now and again – you have got to say to yourself, Well, how am I going to respond to this? I find myself asking for those gifts which are necessary to deal with very difficult situations: faith, courage, wisdom and a right judgement in all things. I believe those things come from God.'

Robin Leigh-Pemberton (Lord Kingsdown) is a former Governor of the Bank of England, an office he held from 1983 until 1993.

A magnificent temple is a laudable monument of national taste and religion, and the enthusiast who entered the dome of Santa Sophia might be tempted to suppose that it was the residence or even the workmanship of a deity. Yet, how dull is the artifice, how insignificant is the labour if it be compared with the formation of the vilest insect that crawls upon the surface of the temple.

Edward Gibbon (1737–94)
from *The Decline and Fall of the Roman Empire*

Vera Lynn

On the eve of the fiftieth anniversary of VE Day, the forces'
sweetheart remains as loyal to the wartime heroes as their
affection for her is undiminished. Reflecting on a lifetime
dominated by those experiences of war, she turns to the words
of a young girl who can sense them only from the memories
of others.

'It is impossible for a young child at that age to have the
emotions that their parents would have had, but they have
learned and discovered a lot about the war. I was in Canada a
few years ago, singing in a concert, and I had some very young
people come backstage to me and say, "Listening to the songs,
and being among the age group that experienced the war, we
learned more about it than we have ever been told." I think it
was because they were all optimistic songs. They were all saying that there would be a better day ahead, and there was
nothing in them that spoke of war, or fighting – none of the
songs were stir-up songs. None of them said "you have got
to fight and win". That is the side that these young people
recognized against the actual fighting, and felt that this was
what had been fought for.'

The poem expresses the debt of gratitude towards those
who laid down their lives.

'Do I echo that? Yes. I felt that I had a compulsion to do
what I have done. It is what I am here for. Although I am not
the kind of person who goes to church every day, I do have
feelings that we are all here for a certain purpose, and I have
felt that this was my purpose – to help and encourage, because
we owe them a debt. I do not see why, just because the war is
over, our appreciation for them should stop. It is lovely that
this child obviously appreciates what she has.'

*Dame Vera Lynn is the singer who became known to
millions of servicemen during World War II through her
radio broadcasts of songs such as 'We'll Meet Again'. She
became known as the forces' sweetheart, and has contin-
ued to work on their behalf ever since.*

I am only a child and it's hard to explain,
The feelings I have, as I sit in the rain,
And I think of the men who went off to war,
Knowing they would not come home any more.

I cannot say thank you to the men left in France,
Who laid down their lives to give me a chance,
I cannot say thank you to the ones who returned,
For thank you is not what those brave men earned.

I owe them my life, as I live it today,
A life lived in freedom because of that day.
I owe them much more than I can every repay,
I owe them the lives that they gave up that day.
They will live in my heart for as long as I live,
And my children will learn of that gift that they give.

Jodie Johnson (aged 9)
The poem, 'Fifty Years Late', was sent to Dame Vera
before the fiftieth anniversary of VE Day celebrations
in 1995

Don Maclean

'It is something that, for several years now, I've written in the front of me diary.' So saying, he breezily whips out the diary to show me. Sure enough, there are the opening words of Psalm 27. 'Basically, if someone asks me what it means to me to be a Christian, then the short answer is, it means never being afraid. I'm not afraid because I firmly believe that God is looking after me personally, and this particular psalm sums it up.'

Don and I have stepped out of the offices of Religious Broadcasting in Manchester for this interview. Curiously, the chance to talk to colleagues about their own beliefs is rare. Even in serious mood, Don's little chuckle never quite leaves him. I ask him about the psalm, a picture of confidence.

'Nobody can harm me so permanently that God will turn his back on me. The word "shrink" is very important to me.' He has the English, rather than the American meaning in mind. 'There are people that you meet in your life, particularly when you are younger, who make you feel as though you are actually shrinking. They are getting bigger and you are getting smaller. They tower over you and they dominate you. But this psalm says to me, No, that is not going to happen. What you have got do to is to think of these words and all of a sudden you will then grow, so that you are exactly the same size as the other people and you can look them in the eye on an equal level.'

'Is there a danger of over-confidence?'

'I suppose it could be dangerous. You could think to yourself, Well I could take risks because it doesn't matter what I am going to do; the Lord is there to look after me and buoy me up. But confidence is so very important. I am not conceited enough to think I've got a hotline to the Lord, but I do think that he has a personal interest in me. And when I was a small child I was incredibly interested in the whole idea of guardian angels. I firmly believed that someone sat on my shoulder, taking instructions from God, being there in place of God to look after me personally. And I still believe that really.'

I ask about the word 'strength'.

'It means inner strength. It is also the strength to strive for what you feel you want in life, and that is not necessarily the material things. I have always had a great desire to be good, since I was a young lad. I have always wanted to do what God wanted me to do, and it's ever so hard isn't it? The path to righteousness is very narrow and it is always uphill, but somehow the thing that you are striving for gives you the strength to carry on, because resilience is the important thing. Again we come back to the word shrink. In your life there are a lot of people trying to domineer us in some way, and then you need your confidence boosted.' He sits back in his chair, to embark on a story.

'About a year ago, I was at a dinner and a chap came over and introduced himself to me. He looked perfectly healthy and in the course of the conversation he said, "I must tell you that I have been told I have only got six months to live." I didn't know what to say on an occasion such as this, so I took me little diary and I said, "Would you like to read this?" And about six months later I had a letter from one of his family who said that, because of the prayer, he was not afraid. He definitely was not afraid – right to the end.'

Don Maclean is presenter of Radio 2's Good Morning Sunday. *He is also a familiar face from pantomime, and from television programmes such as* Crackerjack.

> The Lord is my light and my help;
> whom shall I fear?
> The Lord is the stronghold of my life;
> before whom shall I shrink?
>
> Psalm 27.1
> (The Grail Psalms – numbered
> Psalm 26.1)

Ruth Madoc

'I learned this psalm when I was about six and I loved the imagery in it. It captured my imagination. I lived in Wales for many years and we have a lot of hills, and I think as a child I really felt that God was in the hills.'

'Where do you look to find God now?'

'Everywhere. For me he is universal, and I actually believe that God is in us all. I really believe that. For God to look after me, I have to pray and ask him to listen to my inner thoughts. I do that quite regularly – at least once a day – and I can do it anywhere. Anybody can do it anywhere! That is the one thing I was taught as a child. I went to very many different denominations and all of them had for me this inner core of asking God to listen, and also of you listening to God. Listen to that little inner voice that says, Don't do that. Because whatever time of day or night, he is there for you. I think that is wonderful.'

We move on to the line about the Lord preserving us from evil. I put it to her that there is plenty of evil about, and believers appear not always to be protected.

'Well, we are given the choice. He will preserve us from all evil, I believe, if we want him to. But it is our choice and I know – I believe totally – that the Lord looks after us, if we want him to. My faith is totally unshakeable in this. I am a complete believer and I have no doubt about it. Of course you meet somebody who would try to shatter my arguments totally, but I will not let them, because I say, I'm sorry, I believe in the Lord God.'

She breaks into laughter for a moment, before continuing with good old Welsh passion.

'And you can call him Yahweh, Mohammed, Allah, or you can call him what on earth you like – I don't care. But I actually do try to listen, and it is this listening that is the key. Because if we listen, we will be preserved. Simple.'

Ruth Madoc is well known as a comedy actress, best of all as Gladwys Pugh in the television comedy Hi De Hi. *She has since turned her hand to all manner of shows and pantomime, displaying her talents as a singer and dancer too.*

I will lift up mine eyes unto the hills,
from whence cometh my help.
My help cometh from the Lord,
which made heaven and earth.

He will not suffer thy foot to be moved:
he that keepeth thee will not slumber.
Behold, he that keepeth Israel
shall neither slumber nor sleep.
The Lord shall preserve thee from all evil:
he shall preserve thy soul.

The Lord shall preserve thy going out and thy
    coming in:
from this time forth, and even for evermore.

Psalm 121.1–4, 7–8
(Authorized Version)

Mary Millar

These words changed Mary Millar's life. Before coming to the Christian faith, she suffered long periods of depression. Now, sitting in her little studio at the top of the house, her eyes sparkle as she recalls a memorable sermon she once heard, about the love of Christ.

'It knocked me for six. It was just so amazing. I could see that he did love us so much, and that Jesus did all these things and died. It was as though I were filling up with this marvellous feeling of God's powerful and wonderful love. And I sat, and wept. And I knew at that moment that something had happened to me. Later, I felt that the Holy Spirit had really come into my heart, although I did not really call it that then – I didn't call him the Holy Spirit, because I was still thinking, Oooh, spooky!. But he hadn't come into my head. He was not in my brain because I could not accept that this wonderful, powerful, marvellous God could love me. I was back to me, thinking, I am nothing. A few days later, I was reading my Bible, and I opened it at Psalm 139 and it just leapt from the page, and showed how well he knew me. That all added up – the fact that he knew me so well, really down to the nastiest little bit of me – and in spite of all that, he died for me and he loves me.'

Does it disturb or comfort her to know that God knows so much?

'It doesn't worry me at all. I love it. He is closer to me than my breath. I love the idea that he knows. And when I do go wrong . . .', she leans forward conspiratorially for a moment, 'I'm a terrible gossiper, you know. And if I do gossip about something, then I think, I am really so sorry, I should not have listened to that piece of gossip and I must not pass it on. I know that he knows, so I do not have to hide anything from him. He is ahead of me, so all I have to do is try to catch up.

'I go to him all the time. Isn't it wonderful when we have a friend that we can telephone or meet, and we don't have to put make-up on, or do our hair, and we can just go as we are, perhaps with a problem. They put their arms round us and we can talk as two friends. This is how I feel about the psalm. I feel the Lord is saying, I know you, Mary. He is my best friend. He is closer to me than anybody. I love him very deeply.'

Mary Millar is an actress best known for her part in the television comedy Keeping up Appearances, *in which she plays Rose, the colourful sister of one Hyacinth Bucket.*

O Lord, you have searched me and you know me.
You know when I sit and when I rise;
you perceive my thoughts from afar.
You discern my going out and my lying down;
you are familiar with all my ways.
Before a word is on my tongue
you know it completely, O Lord.
Search me, O God, and know my heart;
test me and know my anxious thoughts.
See if there is any offensive way in me,
and lead me in the way everlasting.

Psalm 139.1–4, 23–24
(New International Version)

Hayley Mills

'It speaks about human beings in a way that I find really inspiring. It speaks of our association and contact with God in a spiritual sense, seeing us as spiritual beings. I heard it put very succinctly once that we are not material beings on a spiritual journey in this life but spiritual beings on a material journey. Certainly the first lines of this poem put that most beautifully for me.'

The actress sits surrounded by her own icons of the spiritual worlds, collected over the years – almost a symbol of her spiritual journey. The poem she has chosen, by William Wordsworth, follows the progress of the soul from infancy to adulthood. First, I must ask what she means by the soul.

'It is the eternal and unchanging element of myself – or of anyone – that is part of God. It is the part of all of us that longs to return from whence we came.'

So to the poem. I pick out the line which reads 'Heaven lies about us in our infancy', and she explains.

'I take that to mean that the baby is closest to God, and as we go through life we often become further and further away. As they put it in the East so well, the veil of illusion becomes denser and denser around us. I believe the baby is very conscious in the womb, and that it probably has consciousness of where it came from. So when a baby arrives it is a miracle, and it is kind of a heavenly being.'

'Have your senses become dulled with time?'

'Well, they did at one time. But hitting forty was a very significant time for me, because it was a time when I began to ask some very serious questions about my life, and where I was going. As soon as you start asking questions again, I think you begin to see the light again, and I do not believe you automatically become shrouded in the darkness of the material world. It can happen, and it happens frighteningly regularly, but it does not have to.'

64

Hayley Mills was voted Number One Star of Tomorrow in the USA and Canada back in 1962. A string of films throughout the 1960s and 1970s followed that accolade and proved the American public right.

Our birth is but a sleep and a forgetting:
The Soul that rises with us, our life's Star,
Hath had elsewhere its setting,
And cometh from afar:
Not in entire forgetfulness,
And not in utter nakedness,
But trailing clouds of glory do we come
From God, who is our home:
Heaven lies about us in our infancy!
Shades of the prison-house begin to close
Upon the growing boy,
But he beholds the light, and whence it flows,
He sees it in his joy:
The youth, who daily farther from the east
Must travel, still is Nature's priest,
And by the vision splendid
Is on his way attended;
At length the man perceives it die away,
And fade into the light of common day.

William Wordsworth (1770–1850)
from *Intimations of Immortality*

James Molyneaux

It is a Tuesday morning when I turn up at the Commons to meet the leader of the Ulster Unionist Party. In the afternoon, Jim Molyneaux is due to see the Prime Minister for talks on Northern Ireland. That afternoon meeting is clearly in his mind, and the prayer he has chosen reflects the suffering of his Northern Ireland. It connects it with all the suffering he has seen: particularly the violence witnessed in his RAF days during World War II.

'It is a prayer which is not used very frequently. It asks that God will be there to relieve in suffering and sadness, and then expresses the sure knowledge – rejoicing in that knowledge – that whatever else may happen, the will of God will ultimately prevail in all circumstances.

'It is an instinctive feeling, in my particular job as leader of a party, that people are looking to one in time of emergency or tragedy. You are conscious that you have to keep your head and suppress your emotions, even at the risk of people feeling that you are unthinking, unfeeling or that you do not care. It is quite the opposite, but there is the conviction that, if one were to go over the top in that kind of situation, you could be destabilizing the situation with unforeseen consequences. And provided that you do not just go through the motions of praying, but deliver yourself into the hands of that higher power, and trust in it, then that does make life possible, which would otherwise be unbearable.'

'Do you ever doubt whether God hears those cries?'

'Well, I am a human being, and sometimes, in a combination of circumstances – for example, if one is not feeling very well, or feeling depressed, and you are suddenly hit with some kind of unexpected emergency – then, like all human beings, there is just a flickering moment of doubt. But the Christian faith very quickly reasserts itself and you recognize and remember that God is still on the throne, that the cry of all of us in tribulation will get a hearing, and that, not only will comfort be supplied, but deliverance will follow.

'I think, after the initial shock – and sometimes fairly quickly after the initial shock – when one attends a service in a village where great suffering and death has been occasioned by terrorism – there is in that simple service, a feeling of inspiration. That is not rejoicing in the suffering or the tribulations, but in the sure knowledge that, however great the odds may be, or the tribulations may be, God will always be there.'

James Molyneaux was Leader of the Ulster Unionist Party, 1979–95.

Almighty and everlasting God, the comfort of the sad, the strength of the sufferers, let the prayers of those that cry out of tribulation come unto thee; that all may rejoice to find that thy mercy is present with them in their afflictions; through Jesus Christ our Lord. Amen.

Book of Common Prayer (1662)
from the service for the sick and suffering

Len Murray

The TUC is not the place for a quiet and relaxing life. As General Secretary, Len Murray had been in the forefront of political argument for a decade. No wonder he has the words of Psalm 46 deeply incised into his memory.

'Refuge is the place where you can get protection, be looked after and cosseted.' The idea sounds so attractive that he smiles at the thought. 'Second, it is a place where you find strength of your own, and can be empowered and enabled. So if, for example, you are at your wit's end, or you are in the middle of a perplexing dispute (as I was sometimes when I was a trades union official) you are able to retreat from that. You know that there is a place you can go to where you can find an inner source of strength. He is there all the time, everywhere, omnipresent and it is a matter of reminding yourself of that.'

'Even when the earth changes and the mountains shake?'

'It does sound cataclysmic, doesn't it? But there is a bottom line, and the bottom line is God's assurance that I will not be moved. In this life you either trust and accept some things, or you are totally at sea. I have never found a situation in which I have been so thrown off that I have utterly rejected the idea of help from God. I have known plenty of situations in which I have wondered whether he is there in spite of all my questioning. So the bottom line is knowing that there is somebody there, and that is an article of faith as much as any other, and more important than most.

'Stillness has played an important part in my life since I started having heart attacks some twenty years ago. When I learned there were times when I had to relax, I found that this process of physical relaxation led me naturally on to thinking about my relationship with and dependence upon God. This psalm reminds us that when you are still, and you go to God and say, Look I am at my wit's end here, God is there. He is always there to help. That help will not be unconditional and it will not be given lightly. God is reminding us that we have duties and obligations ourselves, but that, when the chips go down, and at the end of the road, then God is there. And God *will* help.'

Lord Murray is the former General Secretary of the Trades Union Congress – a post he held from 1973 until 1984.

God is our refuge and strength,
a very present help in trouble.
Therefore will we not fear, though the earth
    be removed,
and though mountains be carried into the midst
    of the sea.
Be still, and know that I am God:
I will be exalted amongst the heathen,
I will be exalted in the earth.
The Lord of Hosts is with us:
the God of Jacob is our refuge.

Psalm 46.1–2, 10–11
(Authorized Version)

Mary O'Hara

By the time she had reached her twenties, Mary O'Hara had already established an international reputation as a singer. After the untimely death of her young husband, her life changed completely. She entered an enclosed monastic order, where she remained for twelve years, only later taking up her distinctive Celtic harp to resume her singing career once again. It would be tempting to fit her own circumstances into an analogy with St Paul's words concerning the mystery of God's purpose. It is a temptation which she stoutly avoids.

'I don't think I can point to moments. I am somebody who lives completely in faith. Nothing approaching a revelation of any kind, however minuscule, has happened to me. In a different realm altogether, I have, for example, no perception of any kind, or any sense of awareness of somebody who has died that I love very dearly. But I know in faith that all is well with them, and that we are united in the communion of saints. But my understanding has been helped by the greater understanding of other people like Paul – I do believe firmly that the Holy Spirit is in operation within each of us and if we let him, he is the one who will do the expanding of the mind, and the understanding not only of the heart but the intellect as well. God has created us with an intellect as well as a heart.'

Paul acknowledges that point too, and encourages his readers to work at their understanding to increase the revelation of God's secret. He says they should do so by binding people together in love. I ask how love and understanding go together.

'I don't really know what the answer is. I know that we must love each other, that God is love, and that "they all may be one, as you, Father, and I am one" – that is Jesus' prayer. If we do what he asks us to do – which is love each other – perhaps that facilitates the understanding, because the Holy Spirit is the love between the Father and the Son. And if, as we are told, our bodies are temples of the Holy Spirit, and we let him operate through us, and let Jesus love others through us so that we end up loving them as he loves them, perhaps that is the doorway. Maybe it is the heart that makes this outreaching of the mind possible.

'Of late I have been very much exercised by the almost incomprehensible truth of the incarnation, that Jesus is true God and true man. He is one of us, and will be for all eternity. And this is what I understand when Paul, as he does in many of his letters, talks about the mystery. That to me is the mystery of mysteries. Sometimes there is this tremendous feeling of gratitude that I have been born when I have been born, not two thousand years before Christ, but two thousand years after his coming on earth. Others have longed to see what we have seen.'

Mary O'Hara is a singer. Her wide repertoire from folk song to contemporary ballad has been heard in most major halls in the English-speaking world, including New York's Carnegie Hall, Sydney's Opera House and London's Royal Festival Hall.

It was God's purpose to reveal the message
which was a mystery hidden for generations and
    centuries
and has now been revealed,
and to show all the rich glory of this mystery
    which was hidden up to now.
The mystery is Christ among you.
I am struggling hard for you to bind you together
    in love,
and to stir your minds
so that your understanding may come to full
    development
until you really know God's secret
in which all the jewels of wisdom and knowledge
    are hidden.

Colossians 2.1–3
(paraphrase)

Daphne Park

The Queen of Spies, as she came to be known, Daphne Park spent the greater part of her career working in the diplomatic service, including assignments to NATO during the 1950s, and later to the former Soviet Union. Her unconventional career was preceded by an equally unconventional childhood which, surprisingly in the circumstances, featured Bunyan's *The Pilgrim's Progress*.

'I was brought up in a very remote part of Africa. We lived in a mud hut in an area where there were lions and where the water was brought once a day from some miles away. There were no telephones, electricity or radio. My mother brought me and my brother up and taught us both with the utmost courage, particularly because she was slowly going blind. It was partly because she was going blind that I learned to read very early and my three favourite books were *John Halifax, Gentleman*, Bunyan's *The Pilgrim's Progress* and Thackeray's *Vanity Fair*. To me *The Pilgrim's Progress* was an exciting story about courage, truth, perseverance and struggle. I admired all those things, and I always have.'

Continuity is one of the themes, based upon the idea that a gift is received, used and bequeathed.

'I look at it, for example, in terms of the continuity of Christian belief in places like the former Soviet Union. It was absolutely vital that somehow the idea of religion should be preserved, and that was why people went to the camps for possessing a Bible and why priests went there for refusing to say whom they had baptized. For them, in those dark days, it was absolutely vital to keep the spark alive. So I tend to see it more in terms of religion in difficult circumstances, than of a normal heritage in a peaceful, civilized, Christian country.

'One of the problems about life today is that we have come to confuse the need to be tolerant with giving up values, and I think the truth, to some extent, consists of being honest with yourself first, and in facing awkward facts.'

'What does it take to be Mr Valiant-for-Truth?'

'Curiously enough, some of the people whom I believe to be the most courageous are very obscure people, who live obscure lives, but live them in courage. Quiet and unrecognized courage on the part of unknown "little" people is a very special kind which I enormously admire, and which goes hand in hand with faith.'

Baroness Park is a former member of HM Diplomatic Service, and was Principal of Somerville College, Oxford from 1980 to 1989.

My sword I give to him that shall succeed me in
    my pilgrimage,
and my courage and skill to him that can get it.
My marks and scars I carry with me to be a witness
    for me
that I have fought his battles who now will be my
    redeemer.

John Bunyan (1628–88)
from *The Pilgrim's Progress*

Colin Parry

The new Secretary of State for Northern Ireland has just met the leader of Sinn Fein for the first time. Two years earlier, such a meeting would have seemed impossible. It was then, in 1993, that Colin Parry came into the public eye for the worst possible reasons. His young son, Tim, was killed by the IRA bomb which exploded in the busy centre of Warrington. Tim was only twelve years old. As I glance round the sitting-room, that innocent smile beams down on me, familiar from a thousand images splashed around the media, which has now forgotten. I read aloud a line from the prayer: 'I want to turn my back, get out, but there stands in my way a cross'.

'These words meant for me that it was very tempting simply to go in on myself and have my family go in on itself – lock the doors, draw the curtains and keep the world out, and grieve privately behind locked doors. But then the cross perhaps meant to me that there was somebody saying, Look, here is a challenge. You have suffered the ultimate pain. You have suffered the ultimate loss, now make something of it.'

'Why the image of a cross?'

'I felt a very fundamental kind of religion when I lost Tim. I am not, by nature, a religious man, but the basics of religion came home to me in a forceful way. The desperate desire that I will see him, hold him and talk to him again one day is absolutely fundamental now for the rest of my life. The help I received from a number of church people at the time was immensely appreciated by me, and if I put all that together it seems that, in my life, which lacked any kind of Christian lead, there was somebody telling me, You can go on, and you can talk and people will listen, so do not waste that opportunity.'

Right now, the prayer's symbol of 'a flower growing on a bombed-out site' is a potent one. Subsequent events would prove optimism for a solution to the Northern Ireland situation to be premature. I ask whether he sees a flower growing.

'I think the flower is the increased chance of normality coming back to a society that has been split apart for so long. It is the image of spring with colour and growth coming from something that has been so black and hopeless for a generation.

I think a flower is the perfect image, and, provided that it is tended and cared for, then there is every chance that that flower will survive and become the symbol for the new Northern Ireland.'

Colin Parry is the father of Tim Parry, who was killed in the Warrington bomb in 1993, aged twelve.

Father, I am a man of my time and situation.
Around me, the signs and symbols of man's fear,
     hatred, alienation:
a bomb exploding in a market square;
faces on TV twisted in mocking confrontation.
I am perplexed, angry, hopeless, sick. I want to turn
my back, wash my hands, save myself, my family,
     get out.
But every time I turn to go
there stands in my way a cross . . .

Lord, make me a child of hope, reborn from apathy,
cynicism and despair, ready to work for that new man
you have made possible by walking the way of the
     cross yourself.
I see a sign, a flower growing on a bombed-out site.
The sign – an empty cross. The burden, Lord, is yours.
Lord, I am a prisoner of hope! There is life beyond death.

A prayer from Northern Ireland

Tony Parsons

'This particular psalm represents the way I feel about my faith. I am not a born-again Christian but someone who rediscovered the faith I had as a child and lost as an adolescent and a young man. I have come back to it, and this psalm – more than any other – represents that journey back to God.'

Tony Parsons' thick East-End accent says something about the man. Other television presenters have toned themselves down to conform to accepted broadcasting norms. Tony seems to tell it exactly as it is. Choosing a psalm which tells the story of a man at a point of utter crying out to the Lord to be saved, begs the question, has he been there too?

'When I was a boy, my father, who was a commando during the war, saw a lot of men die. He was a big war hero – won the DSM. He didn't speak much about the war, but the one thing he did tell me was that when men were close to death, again and again he saw them cry out for God. He saw men that were actually quite godless and atheistic, and people that would have scorned faith, turning to God at a moment when they were approaching death. And I feel, in moments of despair and trouble – and it is most dramatic at the moment of death – you do discover what you believe in. It is easy to forget, because we are so busy. Our lives are so crowded, and our diaries so full, that it is easy to forget the fundamental things that hold our soul together.'

For many people the call to God is answered, just as in the psalm. But others call for help only to find their anguish continues. Is there a chance that this psalm makes it all sound too easy?

'I don't think so. In moments of crisis, tragedy and doubt, people can say, how can God let these things happen? It does literally come down to faith. You have to believe that God is good and full of compassion, and is not responsible for all the evil that men make, and the bad things that men do in the world. So it is a simple psalm and there's nothing wrong with that. I don't think that faith should be a complex or sophisticated thing – you either believe or you don't. And there were times when I had moments of doubt, but I think when you return to the faith that you have always held dear, that you just feel a sense of security and belonging and purpose that you do not have when you are separated from your faith, and from God. My faith is a very simple thing. I believe in God. I had a very simple Anglican upbringing. My family were not overly religious – we tended to go to church to see people get hatched, matched and dispatched. But it always stayed with me what my father said about men on the point of death returning to their faith. And certainly when I have had moments of trouble and strife and sadness in my life, and there has been bereavement, illness, or divorce, I have turned to God in those times to ask for help, and also to thank him for when I felt he was looking out for me. So it is a very simple faith. I believe, and I will always believe and that is a great source of comfort and confidence to me.'

Tony Parsons presents Channel 4's arts programme Big Mouth. *A panellist on BBC 2's* Late Review, *he was for five years a columnist for the* Daily Telegraph *before moving to the* Sunday Mirror *in 1995.*

> The cords of death entangled me,
> the anguish of the grave came upon me;
> I was overcome by trouble and sorrow.
> Then I called on the name of the Lord:
> 'O Lord, save me!'
>
> The Lord is gracious and righteous;
> our God is full of compassion.
> The Lord protects the simple-hearted;
> when I was in great need,
> he saved me.

> Psalm 116.3–6
> (New International Version)

Erin Pizzey

In 1971, the first shelter for battered wives and their children was opened in West London. In the next ten years it gave sanctuary to some 12,000 women, and became a model for similar refuges all over the country. Erin Pizzey, the founder, has a lifelong affinity for those in trouble and need.

'When I am in trouble, which is most of my life, I always go to the psalms of David. He, too, was troubled. He, too, sinned. He was so very human and he had this wonderful relationship with God – very personalized – as did Moses and Abraham.

'All my life, ever since I was three and a half, I have known God personally and I talk to him all the time. If I am not actually talking to somebody else, I am talking to him.'

I stop her for a moment: How can she be so sure of the exact age from which she believed?

'I had this vision when I was three and a half. It was in Africa, and a man was sitting on top of a dead eagle which was burning. He was a wise man – an African wise man – and I pointed at him and he spoke to me. He said that, that night, he would come to talk to me. I was terrified. That night, at about midnight, my twin sister said she wanted to go to the loo. I said, "Please take me to my mother", and she said no, and I rolled up into a ball and closed my eyes. And I heard him calling me – "Erin, Erin".

'I looked round at the window, and there he was – a shining silver light. He talked to me for a long time and told me everything that was going to happen in my life. Then he said, "And now you will forget, but you will always know. Just keep the faith." And that is what I have done all my life.'

That extraordinary story takes the wind out of my sails. After a pause, I ask her where she believes 'the house of the Lord' to be.

She does not pause. 'In the centre of my heart.'

'Is it a place? A feeling?'

'It is a voice. He talks to me. I remember once he said, break this £50,000 contract. Everybody went berserk. "You mean you are going to throw away £50,000?" I said, "I have to, he has told me to", and I did.'

'How do you know it is the voice of the Lord?'

'Because you cannot mistake it. It brings you great serenity and happiness in the face of the most appalling situations. When everyone else would be crying, I am on my knees praying. Even during the dreadful court cases when they tried to jail me. All the way through running this refuge in America, as I passed the staff while we were fighting, I would just say, "Keep the faith, and he will take care of us." Now I am deeply in debt and in terrible trouble, but my heart sings because I am following him.

'I have many enemies. He promised us we would have many, and if I didn't have enemies I would worry, because I would be getting something wrong. You will be hated, he tells us, if you preach my word. I certainly am.'

'So in what ways have you been protected from them?'

'Because they couldn't touch me. I have been shot at in Mexico because I was doing child abuse and paedophile cases, and the neighbours got together and there was violence. They shot my dog on Christmas Day. They attempted to shoot my grandson. They missed! Maybe one day they won't, but that will be God's will, not theirs.'

Erin Pizzey was born in China, captured by the Japanese and became a refugee in South Africa. Much of her life has been devoted to helping women in danger and in need. She has also written several novels.

One thing I have desired of the Lord,
    that will I seek after;
that I may dwell in the house of the Lord all the
    days of my life,
to behold the beauty of the Lord,
and to inquire in his temple.
For in the time of trouble he shall hide me in his
    pavilion:
in the secret of his tabernacle shall he hide me;
he shall set me up upon a rock.

Psalm 27.4–5
(Authorized Version)

Sue Ryder

The pain and suffering she saw as a teenager working in the first aid yeomanry during the last world war has profoundly influenced the life of Sue Ryder. A few years after the war she set up an international foundation for all sick and disabled people to bring relief for those who need it. In that quest she has travelled thousands of miles, but never without a copy of a little poem given to her by her mother. No one seems to know much about its author, Frank J. Exley, but he wrote powerfully about fear, assurance and faith.

'I remember the words spoken or written by a prisoner of the Soviet system, who had been in one of their ghastly gulags, and he said "shut out fear with all strength of faith, then you should have no fear because God is there". And although the prayers may not be answered, he is the person that we must follow every minute of our lives, and be totally guided by him. Fortunately I was born with the gift of faith. It has never really wavered in my life. In the special forces with the Polish section, I had the largest resistance movement in the whole of Europe. They were very young (so was I – sixteen during the early part of the war) and we saw appalling atrocities and situations. They might have had fear, but they never allowed themselves to show it because of their courage and their faith, which I find quite indescribable. And it has gone on like this. I have been with people who are unknown and anonymous, who have shown this tremendous courage and faith, and they have really given me an example to follow.

'I think if one puts oneself entirely in the hands of God then you cannot doubt him. Many terrible things happen and many disappointments. There is always a constant lack of funds for the work of the Foundation in its relief of human suffering. One must have sufficient belief that God, if he so wills, and wants something to come about, will give one the strength to try to do something about it.'

Lady Ryder of Warsaw is founder and social worker of the Sue Ryder Foundation for the Sick and Disabled of All Groups.

Child of My love, fear not the unknown morrow,
Dread not the new demand life makes of thee:
Thy ignorance doth hold no cause for sorrow
Since what thou knowest not is known to Me.

Thy canst not see today the hidden meaning
Of my command, but thou the light shall gain;
Walk on in faith, upon My promised leaning,
And as I goest all shall be made plain.

One step thou seest – then go forward boldly,
One step is far enough for faith to see;
Take that, and thy next duty shall be told thee,
For step by step thy Lord is leading thee.

Stand not in fear, thy adversaries counting,
Dare every peril, save to disobey;
Thou shalt march on, all obstacles surmounting,
For I, the Strong, will open up the way.

Wherefore go gladly to the task assigned thee,
Having My promise, needing nothing more
Than just to know, where'er the future find thee,
In all thy journeying I go before.

Frank J. Exley

Harry Secombe

'When I was a choirboy, which I was from the age of eight until my voice broke (and took a stained-glass window with it), we used to sing this hymn in church, and it became something that we all sang as a family – my brother and I (my brother is a retired vicar) sang it as a duet. So it has always been in my mind and I think music, added to the words, keeps something fresh in your mind.'

I point to the line which reads 'O Lord, support us'.

'Is God a Harry Secombe supporter?' I ask.

'I'm a God supporter! I don't know if he wears *my* scarf! God has been very good to me, and I have been very lucky throughout my life. I went through the wars in the army for seven years and saw a lot of action. People all round me were killed, and I was unscathed, so that is one way he has looked after me. Then I had a very serious operation some years ago, when I had peritonitis, and after I had come through the operation, in Barbados, the surgeon came in to see me, and I said "thank you". "Don't thank me, thank God," he said, which was a nice thing to say. So I think he has been very kind to me.'

'Do you consciously think of the support you may receive from the Lord?'

'Yes, I do. Before I go on stage I say a little prayer. It is almost like a dedication to God, that I am giving my performance to him.'

As the prayer continues, the call for support gets put in the context of a feverishly busy life.

'We all get depressed and downcast. But at the same time, having had that lease of life twelve years ago, when I felt the brush of the angel's wing in no uncertain manner, every day is a bonus for me. Doing the television series *Highway*, travelling around the country meeting people, I was surprised how many people there are doing good without thought of reward, so I do believe there is far more good in the world than we are led to believe by the media.'

'What about the end of the prayer – "the new dawn"?'

'Well, when I was a kid you had this picture of God with a white beard sitting on a cloud and everybody playing harps, but I think there is more to it than that. It is something that happens – there is a serenity, and a peace, and you become part of something that is everywhere. It is not that you are looking forward to popping your clogs, but the older you get the more you look into yourself to see what kind of life you have led and whether you deserve that peace at the last. But I think I will not mind when I have got to go because there is something there. I am not looking forward to it, but I have no fear of death!'

Sir Harry Secombe is one of the popular entertainers of the 1990s, one of the best-known singers of previous decades, and during the 1940s and 1950s was a member of the great comic partnership on the Goon Show.

O Lord, support us all the day long of this troublous life,
until the shades lengthen and the evening comes,
and the busy world is hushed,
the fever of life is over,
and work done.
Then, Lord in thy mercy,
grant us safe lodging,
and holy rest,
and peace at the last;
through Jesus Christ our Lord.

                    Attributed to John Henry Newman (1801–90)

Catrina Skepper

The Cadbury's Flake girl was her first television role. Miss Lean Cuisine, Miss Head & Shoulders and Miss Pretty Polly all came soon after. Catrina Skepper was one of the most photographed faces in the 1980s' fashion and modelling world, appearing not only on television, but also on covers of countless glossy magazines too. But after her huge success in the 1980s she disappeared from view.

'I almost disappeared in more ways than one, because I became anorexic and therefore very thin. I was forced to retire, prematurely probably, from my modelling career, and the next five or six years were fairly bleak. I did not work, I was very ill and looked appalling. I have always had a very strong faith but at this stage it was severely tested because I felt I had turned into an evil person. I had been given all these gifts, and all these so-called successful years of a career. I had a wonderful family, great friends, had travelled all over the world, was earning money – all the things that are the trappings of success – but I managed to get myself into this desperate situation. I would go and sit in the back of the church that I used to go to in London and hardly be able to pray or know what to ask for, because I felt I had failed, and that God was failing me because he was not showing me the way out.

'This poem by Margaret Powers is real to me in a way that is almost too good to be true, because I did have a dream myself. I am not sure whether it was a vision or a dream but it happened during the night. Having gone to bed very cold, lonely and miserable – probably crying – I had fallen asleep. Suddenly I encountered something which cocooned me in this wonderful warmth, and I was lifted out of this terrible state of fear and cold and misery, and taken along a path. I was being carried. I felt weightless and very warm, and it was very bright. Suddenly a voice said to me, "You realize, Catrina, that if you come now you cannot go back." I remember saying, "I haven't finished, I haven't finished", and the voice said, "Well, then you still have work to do." When I woke up I did not dare tell anybody because I thought they would put me in a mental hospital, because at that stage I was very thin – I weighed about five and a half stone. I did not have any blankets over me or anything but I was absolutely warm as toast, and I felt very confident for the first time in a very long time. I realized that even at the times in your life when your faith is severely tested, and when you have little help from friends or people who love you, there is always God, and there is always Jesus ready to carry you across these difficult times.'

Catrina Skepper began her career as a model, later moving into television as a presenter and fashion correspondent.

One night I dreamed a dream.
I was walking along the beach with my Lord.
Across the dark sky flashed scenes from my life.
For each scene, I noticed two sets of footprints
    in the sand,
one belonging to me and one to my Lord.
When the last scene of my life shot before me,
I looked back at the footprints in the sand
and to my surprise,
I noticed that many times along the path of my life
there was only one set of footprints.
I realized that this was at the lowest
and saddest times of my life.
This always bothered me
and I questioned the Lord
about my dilemma.
'Lord, you told me when I decided to follow you,
you would walk and talk with me all the way.
But I'm aware that during the most troublesome
times of my life there is only one set of footprints.
I just don't understand why, when I needed you
    most, you leave me.'
He whispered, 'My precious child,
I love you and will never leave you,
never, ever, during your trials and testings.
When you saw only one set of footprints
it was then that I carried you.'

Margaret Fishback Powers

Una Stubbs

'This was written 300 years ago, and it could have been written yesterday.' She shakes her head and grins. 'All the problems were there then, just as they are now, and life goes on.'

Una Stubbs had suggested we meet up at her agent's, just near Trafalgar Square. Sitting overlooking the Whitehall Theatre, it is enough to get me in the theatrical mood and remind myself of all those plays and films which made her name. *Summer Holiday*, I remember, and *Wonderful Life*. As my mind drifts back a decade or two, hers flits back 300 years, to the words of that nun.

'I think it is the most wonderful piece of wisdom. I first heard it on the radio read by a nun, set to music but spoken very plainly. Then I was working in New Zealand and a technician gave me a copy of it. I pinned it inside my wardrobe door, and have also got it written out in a diary. When I am in turmoil I take myself off quietly and read it through and it calms me down.

'I am basically a placid person but I do have a temper. When it goes the rats can hear me. I can be pretty fiery, but I have a very long fuse, and I do think that if one can keep calm in most situations, it is a very good thing. "Speak your truth quietly to everybody and listen, even to the ignorant and dull for they've got their story too" – I think that is important. If you love human beings, you have got to understand that not everybody has been educated – I do not mean academically, but educated in life and how to conduct themselves. Sometimes people are brusque, maybe because they have a tragedy in their life. It is about trying to understand as many people as possible, and being generous to one's neighbours and the people that you meet.'

I tell her that the poem reminds me a bit of the Book of Proverbs. It has a technique for being wise to the traps and pitfalls of the world, without being cynical about the rest of life.

'I think that is very hard to achieve. Like the ten commandments; they are wise and wonderful, but very hard to achieve. One tries to follow them as much as possible, but ...' She leans forward a little and lowers her voice conspiratorially, 'I don't think of myself as a very religious person, James. I am not. It is just that I do believe in the wonder of nature, the goodness of human beings, the power of love and the power of prayer. There is an over-riding power, but I cannot think of it as a being. If God is love, then that is what I believe in – I really do – and the power of love. And when love is broken down, that is when things go wrong.'

Una Stubbs is an actress known for her stage, film and television appearances. Films she made with Cliff Richard back in the 1960s such as Summer Holiday *and* Wonderful Life *were followed by a range of television hits from* Till Death Us Do Part *to* Worzel Gummidge.

Go placidly among the noise and haste,
and remember what peace there may be in silence.
As far as possible, and without surrender,
be on good terms with all people.
Speak your truth quietly and clearly
and listen to others,
even the dull and ignorant, for they have their
    story too.
If you compare yourself with others,
you may become bitter;
for always there will be greater and lesser persons
    than yourself.
Be yourself;
especially do not feign affection,
neither be cynical about love.
For in the face of all aridity and disenchantment,
it is as perennial as the grass.
Therefore be at peace with God
whatever you perceive him to be.
And whatever your aspirations in this noisy
    confusion of life,
keep peace with your soul.
With all its sham, drudgery and broken dreams,
it is still a beautiful world.
Be careful.
Strive to be happy.

Written by a seventeenth-century nun

John Tavener

'Listen.' The composer needs to explain something, and words will not quite do. He stands up tall and strides slowly towards the piano. I can just see his distinctive flowing hair over the piano lid as he sits at the keyboard, poised to play. He begins to play a chant, harmonizing it in parallel chords. This, he tells me, is why he loves this prayer.

'I remember hearing it in Orthodox services. First of all I was drawn by the extraordinary beauty of the melody. Then, to my wonder, I found the text was also quite extraordinary. It is about paradise, about which we know nothing. The only reason we have for believing in it is because Christ said to the repentant thief, "Today thou wilt be with me in paradise".'

It speaks of one standing outside, unable to go in. Does he recognize himself in that?

'Yes, yes, yes. I am the harlot. I am the thief. I am the condemned; ever in the dark, loving the far-away life. This is my problem with the Western Church – that they seem to have lost any sense of this deep, deep humility and deep sense of repentance – of how worm-like, small and far-away we are from God, who bent the heavens towards the earth.'

So what transforms such a forlorn figure into glory?

'A lot has to do with the depth of repentance, of one's transparency and of one's ability to be able to be as transparent to God. God knows everything, so it does not really seem to matter. But it is important that we are as transparent with God when we speak to him in prayer privately as we are with ourselves. It is important that we are totally ruthless with ourselves in an examination of one day in our lives, or five minutes of our lives. How far are we from God? This is the great paradox with Christianity – and it is the most wonderfully exciting thing – that joy and sorrow can exist side by side in an extraordinary sort of way. The further one feels one is from God, at exactly the same time the nearer one feels. So I would say the transfiguration takes place when I feel far from God – not far from him because he is not near to me, but because I think, "I have no right to be near to him." The more I am able to feel that, the nearer, curiously, he actually is.'

John Tavener is one of Britain's leading composers and many of his works are inspired by his Orthodox faith.

I see thy bridal chamber
adorned,
O my Saviour,
but I have no wedding garment that I may enter there.
Make the robe of my soul
shine,
O giver of light,
and save me.

from one of the so-called bridal chamber services of the
Orthodox Church in which the bridal chamber represents
the heavenly chamber waiting for the believer to enter

Robert Tear

'It is the most buoyant, transcendental passage that shows not only that Paul was in touch with the Holy Spirit in the most extraordinary way, but also that he believed it was possible for everyone to be in exactly that position, and that we should be aware constantly that we are surrounded by goodness and love and the Spirit.

'I have been quite lucky really, because – being acquainted in the small way I am with the spirit of love and goodness – you can never really lose it. So even in the most testing of times one is still surrounded by this great carapace of love. So it seems to me that it is difficult *not* to rejoice in the Lord always. Paul says, once you have rejoiced in the Lord, that is not the end, because you still have to do it again, and again, and again.'

'Are there times when you find it more difficult than others?'

'I don't think so. I am always perfectly aware that I am in the presence of something quite remarkable.'

St Paul's advice is to 'be careful for nothing'. I ask about this.

'It means that if you are being careful for *something*, then you are not concentrating on the Spirit. So once you are obsessed with whatever it might be, the Spirit is being shut out.'

'Is there a danger you could become "careless for everything"?'

'You cannot make the opposite like that. If we are careless for everything, we are also careless for the Spirit, and at that moment we are lost. But we must be careful for nothing because only then can we be inhabited by love.'

Next comes one of the best-known phrases of the Epistles: 'the peace of God, which passeth all understanding, shall keep your hearts and minds through Jesus Christ'. But everyone has their own idea of what is meant by 'peace'.

'Peace occurs when you are careful for nothing, and when you have thrown all your falseness and hopes aside. Then there is only room for the Spirit to enter you and occupy you.'

Robert Tear is one of Britain's most celebrated concert and operatic tenors.

Rejoice in the Lord alway:
and again I say, Rejoice.
Let your moderation be known unto all men.
The Lord is at hand.
Be careful for nothing;
but in every thing
by prayer and supplication with thanksgiving
let your requests be made known unto God.
And the peace of God,
which passeth all understanding,
shall keep your hearts and minds
through Jesus Christ.

Philippians 4.4–7
(Authorized Version)

Margaret Thatcher

'This came to me in a little book of prayers in 1965. I was so impressed with its beauty and with the things that it seemed to echo from my childhood, and my feelings, that I have quietly kept it. When I came to choose my prayer I wanted to choose one which I thought might be slightly different in language, because when you hear something different it jolts your thoughts. Sometimes familiar prayers are *so* familiar that they tumble out without your realizing their full meaning.'

I make mention of the paradox of lost understanding which comes through knowledge and experience. Are there some things the former Prime Minster understood best as a child?

'I think so. Children do have a childlike innocence and trust and dependence upon their parents, if they are brought up in a good home. Indeed, I think today the greatest inequality of all is between those children who have the good fortune to be brought up in a good and loving home, and those who do not have any such experience. So the child brought up like that does have an innocence, a trust and an appreciation of beauty. The laughter of a child is just marvellous. It is that total trust in their parents that has a counterpart in one's trust in God when one gets older. In between, you have to go through that difficult period of testing your own beliefs among your peers. Sometimes you will find you come across brittle cynics who say, "Oh surely you don't believe that stuff – no, don't be a prude like that – you can't believe that at all, it is only what you are taught." And you have to question your beliefs. "Lord, I believe, help thou my unbelief".'

'Has there been a dulling of the spirit compared with the early days?'

'Ultimately, no. I think the questioning leaves you to renew your faith and you come out more strongly having tested yourself. You do not, perhaps, come out quite with the innocence, because your understanding is the greater.

'Your understanding is that we were created in God's image. We have the power and freedom to think, so it is a willingness to pit your own mind against someone else's, and quietly to draw faith from your own experiences. It is about making the leap from reason to faith, and you need your experience to do that.'

Lady Thatcher was Prime Minister of Great Britain from 1979 until 1990.

Let me do my work each day.
May I still remember the bright hours
that found me walking over the silent hills
    of my childhood,
when a light glowed within me
and I promised my early God to have courage
    amid the changing years.
May I not forget that poverty and riches are
    of the spirit.
Though the world knows me not,
may my thoughts and actions be such as shall
    keep me friendly with myself.

Max Ehrmann

Peter Thomson

'Tony Blair's spiritual guru' the tabloids declare. Peter is beginning to groan at the description, and is very pleased that I have come to talk about something other than the part he played in inspiring the Labour Leader's commitment to Christianity in his Oxford days. He moved from his native Australia to North London to be vicar of a densely populated parish in the capital. 'I love it here', he enthuses, taking a couple of coffee mugs, still upside down on the draining board from the Alcoholics Anonymous meeting in the church the night before. He clumps down the kitchen in his big sturdy boots and turns to me with a huge smile to answer my question about the imagery of this prayer.

'This was the prayer that made the most dramatic impact on my life when I was at theological college. Over the forty years of theological education that I have been part of since then, I have come more and more to feel that Jesus' time as a human being, just like ourselves, is crucial to a deeper understanding of one's own religious experience. You feel a sense of oneness with your Lord and Master who deigned to be a carpenter for this significant period of his life.'

'Why is that so important?'

'Because of the identification of Jesus as a human being, which is what I am. It takes away that feeling that Jesus is so separate from our lives that there is no real point of contact. He was doing the kinds of things that his friends, his disciples on earth, are doing every day of their life. When he says such things as "take up your cross and follow me" I understand more what that means. In my own discipleship, this has been very important through the course of my ministry.'

I quote the bit about the rough-hewn wood being fashioned as instruments for God's use. To my next question, he throws back his head and laughs.

'How well worked am I?'

'Pretty smooth?'

'I wish I was – no, pretty rough! We go through this process of discipleship, training, discipline, and what is the true meaning of discipline, other than to be trained into more and more

94

a likeness of what we would want to be and what we were created for, so we can more fully love one another and share that love, and be more vulnerable and open to each other. I have felt myself more and more able to be a participant in God's action in the world, and to become more and more a lover of his creation of which we are a very real part. We need to be perpetually chiselled away at to keep us with that focus.'

The Revd Peter Thomson moved to England to become Vicar of St Luke's, Holloway, after a number of academic posts in Australia.

> Lord Jesus, master carpenter of Nazareth,
> who, through nails and wood, bought man's
>   redemption on the cross:
> wield well thy tools in this thy workshop;
> that we who come to thee rough hewn
> may be fashioned into instruments for thy use;
> who liveth and reigneth with the Father and
>   the Holy Spirit,
> one God forever and ever.
> Amen.

Joanna Trollope

'We are being led on beyond this life, and this is where faith has to take its great leap.' The author's craft is to take the reader beyond that which they know, and help them to leap into belief. But this, surely, is something different.

'You have to be prepared to leap from what you know to what you trust in. One of the glories of this prayer is that it has these enormous concepts, like the resurrection and the life. But then it has this rather practical "bolting it to the earth" as well. It is a prayer on so many levels, from the way you live your Monday to Friday life, to what you aspire to at the end of your life.

'All human beings have a profoundly religious spirit, and I would use that term "religious" in the broadest possible sense. It is that spirit which drives people to strive and struggle to try to improve and enrich things. It does not really matter what labels they give it – whether it is the environment or whatever it is – but in this desire to aspire to something greater than the nuts and bolts of everyday life, is a feeling that there is an inner candle in all human beings.'

Since the prayer makes much of love and fear, I want to know how she understands these terms.

'They are both absolutely vital and inextricable. If you had to choose any one element in life that towers above all the others, it is love. But the fear is necessary to make moral progress. Love is not quite enough – it can get rather uncorseted, shapeless and self-indulgent. The fear is there to whip it into line. I have a little quotation on my desk at home: "Moral progress is the realization that other human beings are fully as human as yourself" – and fear is part of that. It keeps you in check and keeps you polite. I suppose love is the fuel and the energy, and fear is the control.'

'And in relation to God?'

'Exactly the same. The fear is always tempered in my feelings about God with gratitude and praise. But the awe is always there, and mystery, too, is part of the fear of God. I do not believe in the boiling flames or in that kind of stark, crude fear, but in the fear that brings respect.'

Joanna Trollope is the author of The Choir, The Rector's Wife, *and many other best-selling novels.*

O merciful God, the Father of our Lord Jesus Christ,
who is the resurrection and the life;
who hath taught us (by his holy Apostle, Saint Paul)
    not to be sorry,
as men without hope, for them that sleep in him:
We meekly beseech thee, O Father,
to raise us from the death of sin unto the life of
    righteousness; that,
at the general resurrection in the last day,
we may be found acceptable in thy sight,
and receive that blessing, which thy well-beloved
    Son shall then pronounce
to all that love and fear thee, saying,
Come, ye blessed children of my Father,
receive the kingdom prepared for you from the
    beginning of the world.
Amen.

Book of Common Prayer (1662)
from the Burial Service (abridged)

Dorothy Tutin

'The carol has a very beautiful shape. Christina Rossetti sets the scene: the world is so hard, so pitiless and so silent – "snow on snow", "in the bleak mid-winter". She talks about the angels and archangels that may have been there. We do not know for sure. How can we know all these mysterious things that have been described? They are almost myths to us. In the second verse she goes even further, and takes it out of time and space. So when she says "Our God, heaven cannot hold him, nor earth sustain: heaven and earth shall flee away when he comes to reign", you get this sense of absolute endless eternity which our minds cannot really sustain ourselves. And yet we are born to question our own existence. Why are we given this chink in our heads that can say "we exist" but we cannot understand how? Then we want to worship, and it comes down to the child in the manger and the mother's bliss, kissing the child, which, of course, relates to all of us.'

The last verse also deals with the struggle between the *desire* to give and the *ability* to do so.

'Yes, ideally, God should be in everything you do. But I cannot live up to that and I think that is why this moves me so much. I know so well my own total inadequacies. But if you were to live your life with a sense of God all day long – which would be an amazing thing to be able to sustain – you would be able to lead a far better life than I am capable of.

'The lamb I would bring would be those things that are tangible in life – the practical things. If you are an artist or a carpenter – or an actress – you can give your work. But that is only one part of it. That is not you; only the bit of you that does something. But the heart is separate from that. It is the best part of yourself – the purest, the least encumbered. I suppose you will always have a sense, somewhere, of a pure connection that you make with something every now and then. It could be nature, or music. Something very pure is drawn from you, and you do not quite know what it is. But it is so blissful and so lovely. Every now and then it can happen. When you think of things beyond yourself and you are thinking of God and the Spirit, something is drawn from you. It is a thin thread but it is probably the best part of yourself.'

Dorothy Tutin is an actress with a list of stage and film credits simply far too long to summarize. It is enough to say that Stratford-upon-Avon may be considered her natural home.

1
In the bleak mid-winter
Frosty wind made moan,
Earth stood hard as iron,
Water like a stone;
Snow had fallen, snow on snow,
Snow on snow,
In the bleak mid-winter,
Long ago.

2
Our God, heaven cannot hold him,
Nor earth sustain;
Heaven and earth shall flee away
When he comes to reign.
In the bleak mid-winter
A stable-place sufficed
The Lord God Almighty,
Jesus Christ.

3
Enough for him, whom cherubim
Worship night and day,
A breastful of milk,
And a mangerful of hay.
Enough for him, whom angels
Fall down before,
The ox and ass and camel
Which adore.

4
Angels and archangels
May have gathered there,
Cherubim and seraphim
Thronged the air –
But only his mother
In her maiden bliss,
Worshipped the Beloved
With a kiss.

5
What can I give him,
Poor as I am?
If I were a shepherd
I would bring a lamb;
If I were a wise man
I would play my part;
Yet what I can I give him –
Give my heart.

Christina Rossetti (1830–94)

99

Desmond Tutu

'It is such an incredible thing. It turns the world's standards on their head in a remarkable and wonderful way.'

Desmond Tutu has become one of the world's great champions of the cause: turning things on their head is his stock-in-trade. Later, I would meet him at his Cape Town home on the eve of the first multi-racial elections. For now, there is still work to be done, and the words of St Paul provide the inspiration in his quest for true justice.

'This speaks to me because we all seem to be bothered so much by the success ethic, and we think we have to impress God for God to accept us. This passage captures the heart of the gospel which is that God already loves us. God loves me and, even knowing the kind of person that I am, he is willing to give, not this thing or that, but the most precious – his son, his only-begotten son – to die for me. I do not think you can ever find words adequate enough to express the wonder of this gospel.'

Paul finds a lot of them, and expands his thoughts in a complex discourse on justification and reconciliation. But he writes with great excitement, almost as though the full impact of his discoveries is dawning on him as he writes.

'The impact on me is explosive. It means I am able to say that I do not have to do anything to win God's approval. All that I have is gift, and all that I need to do is to accept my acceptance, is to express my deep, overflowing, gratitude for what God has already done for me. And yes, every day I have to be constantly reminding myself that that beggar, that one man who looks like the scum of the earth, is loved with a love that will not change and which will not let them go. That person has a worth that must make me not just respect them, but reverence them.'

Archbishop Desmond Tutu is one the great figures in the building of the modern South Africa. A former winner of the Nobel Peace Prize, he was Archbishop of Cape Town and Metropolitan of Southern Africa from 1986 to 1996. He has subsequently headed South Africa's Truth and Reconciliation Commission.

When we were still powerless,
Christ died for the ungodly.
Very rarely will anyone die for a righteous man,
though for a good man someone might possibly
    dare to die.
But God demonstrates his own love for us in this:
While we were still sinners, Christ died for us.
Since we have now been justified by his blood,
how much more shall we be saved from God's
    wrath through him!
For if, when we were God's enemies,
we were reconciled to him through the death of
    his Son,
how much more, having been reconciled, shall
    we be saved through his life!
Not only is this so,
but we also rejoice in God through our
    Lord Jesus Christ,
through whom we have now received reconciliation.

Romans 5.6–11
(New International Version)

Jean Vanier

'The Magnificat brings together the whole of the message of the Good News of Jesus. This Good News is that each one of us is loved, in all our littleness and weakness. The greatest pain of the poor is the feeling of exclusion; they feel unwanted and therefore no good. The Magnificat shows a vision for those who have been rejected: God is present to them. God is raising them up in love, giving meaning and mission to their lives. The Magnificat is a song of thanksgiving. It gives a vision of God, present in the poorest and the weakest, who then cry out their thanks.'

Jean Vanier has spent most of his life living and working with people who have mental handicaps and who are therefore without privilege or worldly possessions. I ask about the relationship between worldly rank and grace.

'What is important is our attitude to God and to others, not our rank or lack of rank. God can only come to us if we open the door of our hearts. This implies a vulnerability and openness. If we are self-satisfied, closed up on ourselves, we do not need anyone and will not let anyone in. If we are filled with our own glory, then we do not thirst for the glory of God. The cry of Mary is a cry of thanksgiving as she recognizes that God is living in her; and in a very special way because the Word has become flesh in her womb. We too can give thanks and rejoice as we let God enter into our hearts and lives; and God brings us to inner freedom. We are gradually transformed as we receive a new force. God is Emmanuel, "God-with-us", God in us.'

There is a problem in my mind about the reversal of fortunes implicit in the lines which speak of bringing down the rich and exalting the poor. Is it one imperfect balance replacing another?

'Yes, but it is also a question of leading *all* people to salvation and wholeness. The big problem for human beings is around power. We all want to have power, to control ourselves, to control others, and if possible, to control God. But here the cry is that the powerful ones, all those who are closed up on themselves, using power for their own glory, will be brought down. And as they go down, there might be an opening up in their hearts, a cry for help and for love and for God. So they too open up. And if all goes well, everybody in the end will be going up! That is to say, we will all be receiving the gift of God because we will all have been opened up to love and to God.'

Jean Vanier is the founder of the world-wide L'Arche community which began in France to give an ark or safe haven in which people with mental disabilities could live and use their gifts and call people to community life.

My soul magnifies the Lord
And my spirit rejoices in God my Saviour,
For he has regarded the lowliness of his handmaiden.
He has showed strength with his arm,
He has scattered the proud in the imagination of
    their hearts.
He has put down the mighty from their thrones
And exalted the lowly.
He has filled the hungry with good things
And the rich he has sent away empty.

from The Magnificat (Luke 1.46–53)

Wadjularbinna

'Child of warmth and sunshine'. Wadjularbinna, to use her Aboriginal name, was born into the Gungilada tribe of Northern Australia. In England for a mining conference, it is a chance in a million that I come to hear of her. Accepting the invitation to be interviewed is an important step for her. She has a story to tell which she has never told before but which she wants to be heard. It is a personal story which reflects the spirituality of her native people, a fundamental influence despite her early and painful separation from them.

'I was born in a tribal camp. I come from an all-black family and I am the only part-white member of that family. Mama was raped by settlers; to deal with me Mama had to grind charcoal and rub turtle or goanna fat and mix it in with the charcoal and rub it all over my body so that she could cope with me. I ran around with my black sisters and brothers in the tribal camp until the missionaries came and took us away from our parents and put us in an aboriginal community. But there were older girls in the dormitory before I was put in there, so they managed to keep our culture alive.

'The verse from Genesis I have chosen is the very core of our culture. For generations before the white people came to Australia, we had religions of our own and it was all based on the land. We are a part of the land and creation, and that special connection to it begins with conception, when two people go into the bush, choose a spot in the land and call on the spirit to give them a child. My people believe that it is a spiritual transaction which takes place and gives their child a spiritual connection with that land. Non-indigenous people do not understand that we are a part of it. We cannot buy and sell it; we cannot give it away; we cannot destroy it, because it is as though they are destroying our very souls. I believe we have a lot to share and teach non-indigenous people about our spirituality, as we have had to learn from them. I believe in the Lord Jesus Christ because that is the gospel that came to us, and it was sad that the missionaries had to take me away from my parents. The only thing I regret is that I could have heard the gospel sitting on my mama's knee. But they took me away from her. I did hear the gospel, and I will be forever grateful for that. I add it to what I already have in my culture and I would like to think that we could teach them that it is so very important to have beauty around you. And non-indigenous people spend their life working, rushing around, trying to make money, and not having time to talk to somebody they love, or walk in the bush, pick flowers, look at the birds or see beauty around them. Life is too short – it is here and gone.'

Wadjularbinna is an Aborigine. She was taken from her tribe and brought up by missionaries, married a white man and worked on a ranch. Later, she found her natural mother, left her husband and family, and returned to the tribe of her childhood. She still lives there.

And the Lord God formed man of the dust of the ground, and breathed into his nostrils the breath of life; and man became a living soul.

Genesis 2.7
(Authorized Version)

Terry Waite

Knowing his address is proving useless. I have been told to look for the 'Pink House', and yet every house in this small Suffolk village appears to be painted pink. In the end I knock on the door of one of them.

'Sorry, I have no idea.'

'Terry Waite lives there.'

'Oh well, why didn't you say? It's that house over there.'

It is true to say you cannot miss him. He towers over almost everybody, and has the personality (and the laugh) to match. As a former hostage, it must become wearisome to hear the question – what was it like? – but at least I had a reason to ask it. His prayer – written by himself – gives thanks for three gifts: freedom, friendship and food, all denied him during his years of captivity. Did he have to go without, I ask, in order to appreciate these gifts?

'I do not know whether you have to, but when you are deprived, for example, of freedom, and are then in the fortunate position to experience freedom at a later date, it is undoubtedly true that the vast majority of people would experience a new depth and understanding as to what freedom means. Hopefully they will always keep in mind the fact that, in some ways, there is an obligation now on their shoulders to work for the freedom of others.'

Did his relationship with God change when he found himself without freedom?

'In those years of captivity there were times when one desperately wanted conversation – put it like that. And God seemed silent. Totally silent. And it was rather like passing through a dark night of the soul. That is a description that has been used to explain a certain experience of almost non-feeling – not recognizing, nor being able to feel or recognize that there is any God. Those who have successfully passed through that experience will say that the only thing they have been able to do is simply hold on. That was my experience. So what it teaches me, and what is demanded of any individual by God, is to seek out the truth, about yourself, about your nature or about relationships. Even if that truth proves to be personally

106

unpalatable and difficult to bear, pursue it, and the truth will make you free. Would to God that I could always have lived fully in the truth. I have not, and very few human beings do. But I know enough now, as a result of that experience, to say that it is what I want. I hope by the grace of God I shall be able to find it.'

Terry Waite was taken into captivity in Beirut during a mission as the Archbishop of Canterbury's envoy. He remained in captivity for 1,763 days, from January 1987 until November 1991.

> O Lord,
> In a world where many are lonely:
> We thank you for our friendships.
>
> In a world where many are captive:
> We thank you for our freedom.
>
> In a world where many are hungry:
> We thank you for your provision.
>
> We pray that you will:
> Enlarge our sympathy,
> Deepen our compassion,
> And give us grateful hearts.
>
> In Christ's name.

Terry Waite (b. 1939)

Frank Windsor

'It is fairly obvious that we are starting to understand that we are all now totally interdependent. Everything is important and *just as* important.'

Only ten or twenty years ago – the time when Frank Windsor was starring in *Z Cars* and the like – such opinions would be open to derision. Gradually, it seems, the penny has dropped.

'Human beings are not selected to be the chosen few on this earth, so that they and nothing else should survive. If nothing else survives, we will not. That is one certain thing I can say! I love things, I love animals, I love plants, I love to see them. Only this morning we had to say goodbye to a plant because it was dying. We had had it for nearly twenty years, and it had to be taken away. My wife was actually in tears, and that demonstrates the fact that she loved that plant, because she was emotionally connected with it.'

Not only animals, then, but plants too. I read him the part of the prayer which says that to withhold love from any part of God's creation is to withold love from God.

'Can I go so far? Yes. It depends on what your concept of God is, but the unfortunate thing is that so many people think that God is an edified human being. God is totally a mystery. We do not know what God is, but God is there. God is the creator. The problem is that people want to solve that mystery, and we tend to draw God down into a smaller compass. But God is everywhere. It is like that lovely story of the boy whose teacher was talking about the Scriptures and said that God was everywhere.

'"Everywhere?" the boy said, "Is he in this room?"

'"Yes, of course he is in this room."

'"Is he standing by me?"

'"Yes, he is standing right by you."

'"Is he in that inkwell?"

'"Yes, he is in that inkwell."

'So the boy put his hand over the top of the inkwell and he said, "I've got him." You see, that is the childish concept of something which is inexplicable and still a mystery. But he wants to solve that mystery. We have to accept the mystery, not try to solve it. The mystery of God is that he, or she, or whatever, is there in everything that has been created. If we deny the love of anything that has been created, we deny the love of God.'

Frank Windsor is an actor who starred in Z Cars *and* Softly, Softly. *He has appeared in many films and West End plays.*

Lord, may I love all thy creation,
the whole and every grain of sand in it.
May I love every leaf, every ray of thy light.
May I love the animals;
thou hast given them the rudiments of thought
    and joy untroubled.
Let me not trouble it,
let me not harass them,
let me not deprive them of their happiness,
let me not work against thine intent.
For I acknowledge unto thee that all is like an ocean,
all is flowing and blending,
and that to withhold any measure of love from
    anything in thy universe
is to withhold that same measure from thee.

Donald Woods

Everyone who saw the film *Cry Freedom* remembers the South African journalist whose stand against apartheid caused him to be banned and, eventually, flee the country in a style worthy of the Attenborough film his story became. The real Donald Woods now lives in London, but his South African blood is so strong that he asks to read the Lord's Prayer in Xhosa. To those of us used to hearing it in seventeenth-century English, the point brings home the universal and timeless nature of the prayer.

'It encompasses spiritual and, what you might call, political ideals. It talks about the ideal existence. If you have to ask for things, this is what you should ask for – the basics, by which I mean daily bread and so on. But it also says that you should ask to fall into line with the overall cosmic plan, whatever that is.'

We begin to talk about the line 'Thy Kingdom come, thy will be done on earth as it is in heaven.' He cannot resist the temptation to display the beauty of the sound of these words in his native South African tongue. Nor to smile at me triumphantly. But does he think the Kingdom is coming on earth?

'Ya, in its own very slow way the human race since the beginning of recorded history has been stumbling and staggering towards this. There was a time when dungeons were everyday parts of castles, and when slavery was accepted. Slowly, the human race is improving all the time. We might slip back occasionally, but then we keep clawing our way up, like St Peter. Every time you fall you get up again.'

'So why does it happen slowly?'

'I don't know. People have this very simplistic thing that there cannot be a God because there are floods and there are this and that. I always think, how would you explain to Mozart so long ago that one day you could push a button and his symphonies would emerge from a little box? How then can we apply these very simplistic things to such an immense thing as all of creation, and start talking in terms of floods and things as if it is all that easy?'

'Do you forgive those who trespass against you?'

'Ya, but not as well as I should. Not long ago I was asked

110

whether I would want the inquest into Steve Biko's death to be re-opened. Steve Biko was the young black leader who was killed in South Africa. I said, "Yes, it would be good to find out who killed him and precisely how." A short while after that, Nelson Mandela, who had been in prison for twenty-seven years, said, "We have no time to look into the past – we must look ahead." I think that is really a more enlightened view. If this man who suffered so much more than the rest of us can be so unbitter and so uninvolved with digging out who did what to whom in the past, who are we to question that?'

The four policemen responsible for Steve Biko's death confessed in January 1997 to their part in his killing.

Donald Woods is a South African former newspaper editor.

Bawo Wethu (The Lord's Prayer)

Bawo wethu osezulwini, malingcwaliswe i Gama lakho;
(Our father who art in heaven, may your name be held
   in high honour)
mabufike ubukumkani bakho,
(May your kingdom come)
mayenziwe intando yakho emhlabeni njengasezulwini.
(May your will be done on earth as in heaven)
Siphe namhlanje isonka sethu semihla ngemihla.
(To give today our bread, as everyday)
Usixolele izono zethu njengokuba nathi sibaxolela
   abo basonayo.
(Forgive us our sins, as we forgive those who sin
   against us)
Ungasiyekeli ekulingweni
koko sisindise enkohlakalweni.
(Do not lead us into temptation, but liberate us from evil)
Ngokuba bobakho ubukumkani, namandla nozuko
   nangonaphakade.
(Yours is the kingdom, the power and the glory for ever)
Amen.

Acknowledgements

Extracts from the Authorized Version of the Bible (The King James Bible), the rights of which are vested in the Crown, are reproduced by permission of the Crown's Patentee, Cambridge University Press.

The *Revised Standard Version* of the Bible is © 1971 and 1952. Quotations from the *New International Version* of the Bible are copyright © 1973, 1978, 1984 by the International Bible Society. Published by Hodder & Stoughton.

Extracts from *The Book of Common Prayer*, the rights of which are vested in the Crown, are reproduced by permission of the Crown's Patentee, Cambridge University Press.

The hymn by James Quinn, which appears on page 35, is reproduced by permission of the publishers, Geoffrey Chapman.

The publishers and author have made every attempt to contact copyright holders for the use of material in this book. If copyright material has been used inadvertently without permission, the publishers would be delighted to hear from those concerned.

Index

of authors and references to prayers

The Society for Promoting Christian Knowledge (SPCK) has as its purpose three main tasks:

- **Communicating the Christian faith in its rich diversity**

- **Helping people to understand the Christian faith and to develop their personal faith**

- **Equipping Christians for mission and ministry**

SPCK Worldwide serves the Church through Christian literature and communication projects in over 100 countries. Special schemes also provide books for those training for ministry in many parts of the developing world. SPCK Worldwide's ministry involves Churches of many traditions. This worldwide service depends upon the generosity of others and all gifts are spent wholly on ministry programmes, without deductions.

SPCK Bookshops support the life of the Christian community by making available a full range of Christian literature and other resources, and by providing support to bookstalls and book agents throughout the UK. SPCK Bookshops' mail order department meets the needs of overseas customers and those unable to have access to local bookshops.

SPCK Publishing produces Christian books and resources, covering a wide range of inspirational, pastoral, practical and academic subjects. Authors are drawn from many different Christian traditions, and publications aim to meet the needs of a wide variety of readers in the UK and throughout the world.

The Society does not necessarily endorse the individual views contained in its publications, but hopes they stimulate readers to think about and further develop their Christian faith.

For further information about the Society, please write to:
SPCK, Holy Trinity Church, Marylebone Road,
London NW1 4DU, United Kingdom.
Telephone: 0171 387 5282